THE WORLD BOOK

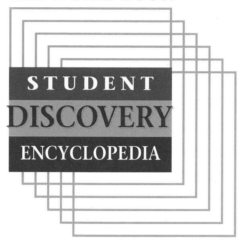

STUDENT
DISCOVERY
ENCYCLOPEDIA

THE WORLD BOOK

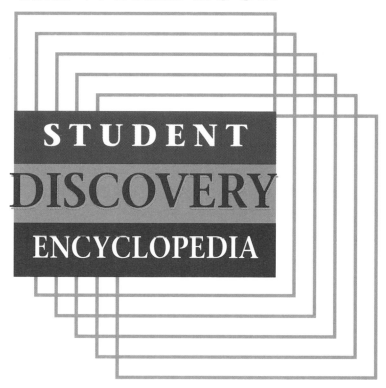

STUDENT

DISCOVERY

ENCYCLOPEDIA

I·J
K·L

6

World Book, Inc.

A Scott Fetzer company

Chicago

For information on other World Book products,
visit our Web site at **http://www.worldbook.com**

For information on sales to schools and libraries,
call **1-800-975-3250.**

●　●

World Book, Inc.
233 N. Michigan Ave.
Chicago, IL 60601

Library of Congress Cataloging-in-Publication Data

The World Book student discovery encyclopedia.
    p. cm.
    Contents: v. 1. A — v. 2. B — v. 3. C — v. 4. DEF — v. 5. GH — v. 6. IJKL —
v. 7. M — v. 8. NO — v. 9. PQR — v. 10. S — v. 11. TU — v. 12. VWXYZ — v.
13. Index.
    Summary: A general elementary encyclopedia with brief illustrated articles
covering an alphabetical array of topics.
    ISBN 0-7166-7400-9
    1. Children's encyclopedias and dictionaries. [1. Encyclopedias and
dictionaries.] I/ World Book, Inc.
AG5.W838   2000
031—dc21   99-37393
                                                                          CIP
                                                                          AC

Printed in the United States of America
1 2 3 4 5 6 7 8 9 06 04 03 02 01 00 99

Acknowledgments

● ●

The publishers gratefully acknowledge the courtesy of the following artists, photographers, publishers, institutions, agencies and corporations for the illustrations in this volume. Credits should be read from top to bottom, left to right on their respective pages. All maps and all entries marked with an asterisk (*) denote illustrations that are the exclusive property of World Book, Inc. Artwork for all country flags was adapted from Cliptures™ by Dream Maker Software. State and province flags and seals were provided by the Flag Research Center unless otherwise credited. Artwork for state and province birds and floral emblems was provided by John Dawson*. History artwork for the states and province articles was provided by Kevin Chadwick*.

11 Steven Liska*

12-13 Jan Wills*; © David Young-Wolff, PhotoEdit; Eileen Mueller Neill*

14-15 Bressler Ice Cream Company (WORLD BOOK photo*); © Soenar Chamid, Tony Stone Images; Robert Keys*

16-17 David Cunningham*; © James R. Holland; Marion Pahl*

18-19 © David R. Frazier

20-21 © Artstreet

22-23 © Cathy Melloan; © Chuck Fishman, Woodfin Camp, Inc.; © David R. Frazier; © Phillipe Plailly/SPL from Photo Researchers

24-25 © Juergen Berger, Max Planck Institute/SPL from Photo Researchers; © Alan & Sandy Carey, Photo Researchers; © Two Sisters (On the Terrace) (1881) oil on canvas, The Art Institute of Chicago, Mr. & Mrs. Lewis Larned Coburn Memorial Collection; Richard Hook*

26-27 Statues about 2" (5 cm.) high; Field Museum of Natural History (WORLD BOOK photo*); © Victor Englebert; © Ron Sherman, Tony Stone Images

28-29 WORLD BOOK photo by David Frazier*

30-31 © Cathy Melloan; © Superstock

32-33 Richard Hook*; Richard Hook*; Michael Hampshire*; John Dawson*

34-35 © Jerry Jacka; Charles McBarron*; © Scott Blackman, Tom Stack & Associates; © Wilbur Montgomery, Eiteljorg Museum

36-37 Attack at Dawn (about 1900) oil on canvas by Charles Schreyvogel, the Thomas Gilcrease Institute of American History and Art, Tulsa, OK

38-39 © Gene Ahrens, Superstock

40-41 © Byron Crader, Ric Ergenbright Photography

42-43 © Manfred Gottschalk, Tom Stack & Associates; Engraving (about 1835) by an unknown artist; Illustration from An Introduction to the Industrial and Social History of England, (Newberry Library, Chicago); Lithograph by Englemans; La Vie du Rail Magazine, Paris

44-45 © Internationale Bilderagentur; © Mark Adams, FPG; © Lori Adamski Peek, Tony Stone Images

46-47 Granger Collection; Tom Dolan*; Tom Dolan*; Tom Dolan*

48-49 © Alexander B. Klots; Eileen Mueller Neill*; Tom Dolan & James Teason*; Sandra Doyle, Wildlife Art Ltd.

50-51 James Teason*; Richard Hook*; © Tony Stone Images; © Penny Gentieu, Tony Stone Images

52-53 © Superstock; © David R. Frazier Photolibrary; © Porterfield-Chickering, Photo Researchers; © David M. Dennis, Tom Stack & Associates

54-55 Eileen Mueller-Neill*; © Bryan & Cherry Alexander

56-57 © P.H. Cornut, Tony Stone Images; Marion Pahl*; Marion Pahl*; Marion Pahl*

58-59 Lydia Halverson*; Lydia Halverson*; James Teason*; John F. Eggert*; Tom Dolan*

60-61 © Cathy Melloan

62-63 © Georg Gerster, Photo Researchers

64-65 © Ric Ergenbright Photography

66-67 © Superstock; © Filip Horvat, Saba

68-69 © Tony Stone Images

70-71 WORLD BOOK photo*; © Richard Lobell; © Superstock

72-73 © Nabeel Turner, Tony Stone Images; Paul Turnbaugh*; Paul Turnbaugh*; Paul Turnbaugh*

74-75 © Bob Ivey, Ric Ergenbright Photography

76-77 © Richard Lobell

78-79 © Earl Roberge, Photo Researchers; © Joe Cornish, Tony Stone Images

80-81 Netsuke (1700's-1800's); Seattle Art Museum, Duncan MacTavish Fuller Memorial Collection (Paul Macapia); Horse (about 20,000 B.C.), Musée des Antiquites Nationales, St. Germain-en-Laye, France; Ivory Diptych with Apostles (about A.D. 500), Christian Museum, Brescia (SCALA/Art Resource)

82-83 Detail of an oil painting (about 1832) by Ralph E. W. Earl, collection of the Daughters of the American Revolution Museum, Washington, D.C.; Chicago Historical Society

84-85 © Reuters/Archive Photos; © Mark Burnside, Tony Stone Images; Paul Lopez*; © Superstock

86-87 © Ric Ergenbright

88-89 © Steve Vidler, Tony Stone Images

90-91 © Orion Press from The Stock House; © David Redfern, Retna; © Jack Vartoogian;

92-93 © Jack Vartoogian; © Duncan P. Scheidt; Granger Collection; © Mark Burnett, David R. Frazier Photolibrary

94-95 © Brian Parker, Tom Stack & Associates; NASA; © George Chan, Photo Researchers

96-97 George Suyeoka*; © Charles Harbutt, Magnum

98-99 Isidre Mones*; George Suyeoka*

100-101 © Travelpix from FPG; Tennessee Historical Society; © Stephen Dunn, Allsport

102-103 © Malak Karsh, Photo Researchers; Corbis/UPI; Granger Collection; © Archive Photos

104-105 © C. Ferrare, Imapress from NSP

106-107 AP/Wide World; Corbis/Bettmann

108-109 © Bill Aron, Tony Stone Images; Julian Research Institute; Joan Holub*

110-111 Lowell Hess*; Pat & Robin Dewitt*; Precision Graphics*; Herb Herrick*

112-113 NASA/JPL; Andrew McGuire; © Paolo Koch, Photo Researchers

114-115 Self-portrait with Thorn Necklace and Hummingbird (1940) oil on board by Frida Kahlo, Collection of the Harry Ransom Research Center, University of Texas, Austin; © Dick Loftus; © Cathy Melloan; Jean Cassels*

116-117 © Jim Patrico, David R. Frazier Photolibrary

118-119 Corbis/Bettmann

120-121 Corbis/UPI; © CNP/Archive Photos; AP/Wide World

122-123 © William Strode, Woodfin Camp, Inc.

124-125 © W. Perry Conway, Tom Stack & Associates

126-127 © William S. Weems, Woodfin Camp Inc.; Portrait by an unknown artist, collection of Mrs. John T. Wainright (WORLD BOOK photo*); Benson Studios*; Mary Ann Olson & Paul Peck*

128-129 © Daryl Balfour, Tony Stone Images; James Teason*; © Victoria Beller-Smith from E. R. Degginger; Granger Collection; AP/Wide World

130-131 AP/Wide World; © Consolidated News/Archive Photos; Detail of a portrait by Frank O. Salisbury, House of Commons, Ottawa (John Evans)

132-133 Lydia Halverson*; Benson Studios*

134-135 James Teason*; From A Boy's King Arthur by Sidney Lanier, illustrated by N.C. Wyeth © 1917 by Charles Scribner's Sons. Used by permission of the publisher; Allan Phillips*

136-137 Lydia Halverson*; Express Newspapers/Archive Photos; Jean Helmer*; Eileen Mueller Neill*

● Acknowledgments

138-139 WORLD BOOK illustrations*; Stan Galli*; Simon & Schuster Children's Publishing

140-141 Harry McNaught*; AP/Wide World

142-143 © Superstock

144-145 © Korean National Tourist Office; © Manfred Gottschalk, Tom Stack & Associates

146-147 Ministry of Culture & Information, Seoul, South Korea

148-149 © Lawrence Migdale, Photo Researchers; © Sylvain Grandadam, Tony Stone Images

150-151 © Cathy Melloan; AP/Wide World

152-153 Pamela G. Johnson*; Granger Collection; © Dave Schiefelbein, Tony Stone Images

154-155 © L.L.T. Rhodes, Tony Stone Images; © Cathy Melloan

156-157 © Cathy Melloan; © David Stover, Uniphoto; © Robert E. Daemmrich, Tony Stone Images

158-159 National Archives of Quebec

160-161 © Andy Levin, Photo Researchers; © Chuck O'Rear, Corbis/Westlight; Benson Studios*

162-163 Benson Studios*; NASA; © Phil Degginger, Tony Stone Images; Coherent General, Inc.

164-165 © Paul Meredith, Tony Stone Images

166-167 Detail of a portrait by John Russell; House of Commons, Ottawa (John Evans); Illuminated Manuscript (about 1450) by an unknown English artist; Granger Collection; © Robert E. Daemmrich, Tony Stone Images

168-169 Eileen Mueller Neill*; WORLD BOOK photo*; James Teason*; WORLD BOOK photo*

170-171 James Teason*; © J. M. Charles, Photo Researchers; WORLD BOOK photo by Ralph Brunke*

172-173 © Gianni Tortoli, Photo Researchers

174-175 Granger Collection; Brown Brothers; Robert Demarest*; Kate Lloyd-Jones, Linden Artists Ltd.*

176-177 © Kenneth W. Fink, NAS from Photo Researchers; Precision Graphics; *Mona Lisa* (1503) oil on wood, The Louvre, Paris (Giraudon/Art Resource); *Self portrait* (about 1514) red chalk by Leonardo da Vinci; Biblioteca Reale, Turin, Italy (SCALA/Art Resource)

178-179 From the *Codex Atlanticus* fol. 311v., Biblioteca Ambrosiana, Milan, Italy (SCALA/Art Resource); WORLD BOOK illustration*

180-181 Carol A. Brozman*; Granger Collection; © Hulton Getty from Liaison Agency

182-183 © Artstreet

184-185 Oak Park Elementary Schools (WORLD BOOK photo by Dan Miller); WORLD BOOK photo; © Bernard Boutrit, Woodfin Camp, Inc.; © David R. Frazier, Photo Researchers; WORLD BOOK photo*

186-187 WORLD BOOK photo*; WORLD BOOK photo*; Granger Collection; Detail of a German engraving (1800's) from the Granger Collection

190-191 Laura D'Argo*

192-193 Roberta Polfus*; © Cathy Melloan; © James E. Lloyd, University of Florida

194-195 WORLD BOOK photo by Terry Renna*; Eileen Mueller Neill*; © R.L. Goddard, Berg & Associates; United States Lighthouse Society

196-197 © Ralph Welmore, Tony Stone Images; WORLD BOOK illustration*; Robert Hynes*; *Boyhood of Lincoln* (1868) oil on canvas by Eastman Johnson; University of Michigan Museum of Art, Bequest of Henry C. Lewis

198-199 Granger Collection; AP/Wide World; Culver Pictures

200-201 © Norman Myers; © Purdy Matthews, Tony Stone Images; © Cathy Melloan

202-203 Lucinda McQueen*; Illustration by Ed Young. Reprinted by permission of Philomel Books from *Lon Po Po, A Red Riding Hood Story from China* © 1989 by Ed Young; Elizabeth Miles*; From *Cezanne Pinto*: A Memoir by Mary Stoltz © 1994 by Mary Stoltz. Reprinted by permission of Alfred A. Knopf, Inc.

204-205 Reprinted by permission of G.P. Putnam & Sons. *Dragonflies* by Oxford Scientific Films. Text © 1980 G. Whizzard Publications Ltd. Illustration © 1980 by Oxford Scientific Films; Karen Loccisano*; Jan Brett*; Pat Traub*

206-207 © Charles Thatcher, Tony Stone Images; Robert Demarest*

208-209 WORLD BOOK illustration*; Richard Lewington, The Garden Studio*; John F. Eggert*; Roberta Polfus*; Pat & Robin Dewitt*; © George H. Harrison; Bruce Coleman Inc.

210-211 David Wenzel*; Benson Studios*; Benson Studios*; © Gianni Tortoli, Photo Researchers; Shirley Hooper, Oxford Illustrations Ltd.*

212-213 Gonzalez Vicente, S. I. International*; © Alan Kearney, FPG; © Thomas Kitchin, Tom Stack & Associates

214-215 © Doug Armand, Tony Stone Images; Folger Shakespeare Library; A sketch by Franquinet, The Longfellow House, Cambridge, Mass.

216-217 WORLD BOOK diagram*; © Craig Jones, Allsport; © Chad Ehlers, Tony Stone Images

218-219 © Terry Qing, FPG

220-221 Carol A. Brozman*; © Reuters/Archive Photos; Joe Van Severen*

222-223 Sharon Ellis*; Granger Collection

Key to pronunciation

● ●

The World Book Student Discovery Encyclopedia provides pronunciation for many unusual or unfamiliar words. In the pronunciation, the words are divided into syllables and respelled according to the way each syllable sounds. The syllables appear in *italic* letters. For example, here are an article title and the respelled pronunciation for it:

Diplodocus (*duh PLAHD uh kuhs*)

The syllable or syllables that get the greatest emphasis when the word is spoken are in capital letters (*PLAHD*).

The World Book Student Discovery Encyclopedia uses a number of special characters and marks to give the correct spellings for many words and names in languages other than English. These marks have various meanings, according to the languages in which they are used. An acute accent mark (´) over an *e* in a French word indicates that the *é* is said *ay*. An acute accent mark over an *e* in a Spanish word indicates that the syllable containing the *é* has the main emphasis in the word.

The pronunciation key at the right shows how common word sounds are indicated by marks in *The World Book Dictionary* and by respelling in *The World Book Student Discovery Encyclopedia*. The key also shows examples of the *schwa*, or unaccented vowel sound. The schwa is represented by ə.

Letter or mark	As in	Respelling
a	h*a*t, m*a*p	a
a	*a*ge, f*a*ce	ay
ã	c*a*re, *ai*r	ai
ä	f*a*ther, f*a*r	ah
ch	*ch*ild, mu*ch*	ch
e	l*e*t, b*e*st	eh
e	*e*qual, s*ee*, ma*ch*ine, cit*y*	ee
er	t*er*m, l*ear*n, s*ir*, w*or*k	ur
i	*i*t, p*i*n, h*y*mn	ih
i	*i*ce, f*i*ve	y or eye
k	*c*oat, loo*k*	k
o	h*o*t, r*o*ck	ah
o	*o*pen, g*o*, gr*o*w	oh
ô	*o*rder, *a*ll	aw
oi	*oi*l, v*oi*ce	oy
ou	h*ou*se, *ou*t	ow
s	*s*ay, ni*c*e	s
sh	*sh*e, va*c*ation	sh
u	c*u*p, b*u*tter, fl*oo*d	uh
u̇	f*u*ll, p*u*t, w*oo*d	u
ü	r*u*le, m*o*ve, f*oo*d,	oo
	m*u*sic	yoo
zh	plea*s*ure	zh
ə	*a*bout, *a*meba, tak*e*n, p*u*rple, pen*c*il, lem*o*n, circ*u*s, curt*ai*n, Egypt*i*an, sect*io*n, danger*ou*s	uh

How to use *The World Book Student Discovery Encyclopedia*

- Thousands of illustrations
- Guide words
- Phonetic spellings
- Related article lists
- Clear cross-references
- Fact boxes and timelines
- Special feature articles
- Hands-on activities

The World Book Student Discovery Encyclopedia is a general encyclopedia. It has information about people, places, things, events, and ideas. Entries are written in a way that makes them easy to understand.

Finding entries is easy, too. They are arranged in alphabetical order. There is also an index in volume 13. The index lists all the entries, as well as topics that are covered in the set but that are not themselves entries. Volume 13 has an atlas, too. It features maps of the world and maps of individual continents. Over 400 other maps are found throughout the set.

The many features of *Student Discovery* make it an encyclopedia that you can use for research as well as read just for fun.

Guide words At the top of each page is a guide word. Guide words help you quickly find the entry you are seeking.

● Earth Day

Earth Day

Earth Day is celebrated on April 22. It is a special day set aside every year to remind people to take care of the environment. The environment is all the things on Earth that support life—the air, water, and land. On Earth Day, millions of people all over the world gather to clean up their communities. They also protest threats to the environment and celebrate progress in cutting down pollution.

Earth Day was first celebrated in the United States in 1970. That year, the U.S. Congress formed the Environmental Protection Agency. Congress also passed the Clean Air Act of 1970. This law said that cars and factories had to limit the amount of air pollution they could give off. Other new laws followed.

The first Earth Day was celebrated in April 1970.

Earth science

Earth science is the study of Earth. Earth scientists try to find out how Earth began and how it has changed. They study what Earth is made of. They study the atmosphere (*AT muh sfihr*). The atmosphere is the layer of gases—including air—that surrounds Earth. They also study the oceans and seas.

Earth scientists learn about Earth's crust and rocks through the science of geology (*jee AHL uh jee*). Meteorology (*mee tee uh RAHL uh jee*) helps them understand the earth's weather and climate. The science of oceanography (*oh shuh NAHG ruh fee*) helps them study the oceans. They learn about mountains, rivers, seas, and other parts of Earth through physical geography (*FIZ uh kuhl jee AHG ruh fee*).

Other articles to read: **Geology**; **Paleontology**.

A satellite picture of a storm over Europe helps earth scientists called meteorologists study the weather.

Earthquake

An earthquake is the shaking of the ground caused by movements in the earth. Earthquakes happen when large sections of the earth's rocky outer shell—called the crust—suddenly break and shift. Earthquakes are among the most powerful events on the earth. They can cause great damage and loss of life.

Most earthquakes happen along a break in the earth's crust called a fault. Movements in the crust put stress on large blocks of rock along a fault. This stress bends the rock. Over time, the stress on the rock becomes so great that the rock breaks. Suddenly, the rock snaps into a new position. This causes the ground to shake.

When an earthquake happens, the breaking rock sends a burst of energy through the earth. The energy travels in the form of vibrations, which are back and forth movements. These movements are called seismic (*SYZ mihk*) waves. Seismic waves move out from the middle of the earthquake in all directions. Rock movements during an earthquake can shake buildings and even cause them to fall down. Roads and highways may crack. Bridges may fall down. Hillsides may break loose and tumble down. Rivers may even change their course. A large earthquake beneath the ocean can create huge waves that reach the shore. These waves, called tsunamis (*tsoo NAH meez*), can flood coasts for miles.

Other articles to read: **Plate tectonics**; **Tsunami**.

Earthquakes can cause r highways to crack and bri

Along faults, blocks of in three main ways. They apart *(above)*. Or, they m together or slide past ea

Earthworm. See Worm.

Pronunciations The phonetic spellings for many unusual or unfamiliar words are given. A key to the pronunciation is in the front of each volume.

Cross-references The cross-references appear in heavy type—the same as article titles. For example, there is a cross-reference from **Earthworm** to **Worm.** This means if you look up **Earthworm,** you will be told to see the **Worm** article.

Related references The references at the bottom of many articles tell you what other articles to read to find out more or related information.

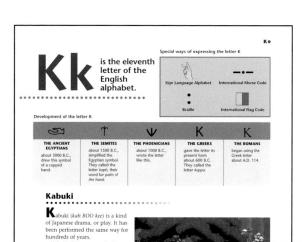

Features on letters of the alphabet
Each letter of the alphabet has an article explaining its history. The article also shows special ways of expressing that letter.

Section headings Many articles of two or more pages are divided into sections. Each section has its own heading. Headings appear in **boldface** type and tell you what information will be found in the section.

Kabuki

Kabuki (*kah BOO kee*) is a kind of Japanese drama, or play. It has been performed the same way for hundreds of years.

Kabuki plays are popular in Japan. Some of them are about history, and others are about people in everyday life. The scenery is beautiful, and the actors wear colorful costumes and makeup. The acting in kabuki plays is very lively. Chanting and music are part of the plays.

Kabuki began in the 1600's. Some of its style was copied from puppet plays, which were very popular. In kabuki theater, men play all the parts.

Kabuki actors wear colorful costumes and makeup.

● City

City

Cities are places where thousands or even millions of people live and work. Cities are the world's most crowded places. Around the world today, between two-fifths and one-half of the people live in cities. In the United States, three-fourths of the people live in cities.

The parts of a city
Many of today's big cities have a central section called the downtown area. The downtown area has department stores, banks, museums, and government buildings, as well as the main offices of big companies. Many people who travel downtown to work live in city neighborhoods or in suburbs. Suburbs are communities that lie outside the city. An industrial region of factories and other buildings often lies just outside the downtown area. The neighborhoods where people live are usually outside the industrial region. The oldest and most run-down neighborhoods are often the neighborhoods closest to the city center. This area is called the inner city. Newer neighborhoods lie farther away from the inner city. The newest neighborhoods are in the suburbs.

Life in a city
Cities offer many things for people to do. People can go to art museums to see paintings, sculptures, and other works of famous artists. They can listen to music at concerts and see movies from around the world. They can eat at restaurants that serve food from many different cultures. They can shop at big department stores. They can cheer their favorite sports teams at huge stadiums.

Skyscrapers tower over the busy streets of Bogotá, Colombia.

Most people choose to live in or near cities because they can find many different jobs there. Cities in most modern countries have businesses and factories that make all kinds of products. These businesses provide jobs for many people. Less modern cities, in countries such as Africa, Asia, and Latin America, have far fewer jobs. Even so, large numbers of people flock to these cities hoping to find work.

Problems of cities
Many cities are overcrowded, dirty, and noisy. Traffic jams make trips to work and other places long and slow. Cars and factories pollute the air and harm people's health. Cars and trucks, factories, sirens, and building equipment make a lot of noise. And there is usually more crime in many cities than in suburbs or farm areas. Violence sometimes breaks out between groups of people of different races or religions. People have worked to solve these problems, but much more needs to be done.

Other articles to read: **Community; Neighborhood; Suburb.**

City ●

This painting shows the old English city of Bath.

City parks, like this one in Chicago, Illinois, have flowers and fountains for people to enjoy.

Many companies have offices in big cities like London.

104 The World Book Student Discovery Encyclopedia

The World Book Student Discovery Encyclopedia 105

Illustrations Each article in *Student Discovery* is illustrated. There are over 3,500 photographs, drawings, maps, and other illustrations in the set. Each of them is labeled or explained in a caption.

● Book

Book

Books are written or printed on sheets of paper that are fastened together along one edge. A cover protects these pages. Books help people find knowledge and information. For this reason, the book is one of the world's greatest inventions.

Young people read storybooks, schoolbooks, workbooks, and comic books. For information, people often look in almanacs, dictionaries, encyclopedias, and telephone books. For entertainment, we read poetry, plays, and long stories called novels.

The pages of a book are glued or sewed together along one side, called the spine. The cover is joined to the spine. The book title and other information appear on the spine and cover.

Nobody knows exactly when the first books appeared. We do know that people have used books in some form for more than 5,000 years. In ancient times, people wrote on clay tablets, on strips of wood, or other materials. Books that had pages began to appear about 2,000 years ago.

At first, all books were written by hand, one at a time. The Chinese made the first known printed book about 1,100 years ago. They carved each page from a block of wood. Then they spread ink over the raised surfaces on the wood and printed it on

An illuminated manuscript, such as the one above, is a book written and decorated by hand.

This diagram shows the main steps in binding a hardcover book by machine. First, the sheets of paper are folded into pages. The folded sheets, called signatures, are sewed together in their correct order. The spine of the sewed book is shaped into a curve. This is called rounding. Then a hinge is made on each side of the spine. This is called backing. A lining of strong fabric called a super is glued to the spine. Finally, the book is joined to its cover, called the case. This is called casing-in.

paper. In this way, they could make many copies of a book.

The books we have today began with the invention of movable type. In movable type, each letter of the alphabet is a separate piece of metal. Printers can place the metal type in any combination to produce the words they want. In the 1400's, a German named Johannes Gutenberg was the first printer in Europe to print books with movable type. By the early 1500's, printing had spread throughout Europe. Since then, millions of books have been printed on almost every subject and in every written language.

Other articles to read: **Library; Literature for children; Printing; Type.**

HANDS-ON!

Bind Your Own Book

Do you have some pages you would like to make into a book? Collect the pages of your book in order. To make the cover, cut two pieces of thicker paper, or cardboard, the same size as the pages. Cut a strip of paper 1 inch (2.5 cm) wide and just as long as your cover. Use a single-hole punch to make holes in the strip about ¼ inch (.75 cm) from the side, and ½ inch (1.25 cm) apart from each other. This strip will be used as a guide.

Place the guide over the far left side of the front- and back-cover pages and punch holes where there are holes in the guide. Take groups of pages from the inside of the book and punch holes in the same way until all the pages are done.

Now thread a piece of twine (thick thread) through the holes from the top, leaving a 6-inch (15 cm) tail. Then loop the twine under the bottom, and thread again through the holes from the bottom. Tie the two tails in a knot.

To hide the stitches, fold a 1½-inch (4 cm) piece of colored tape over the edges of the front and back cover, centering it on the "spine" of the book. The spine is the place where the pages are fastened together. Press over the stitching, then trim tape to same length as top and bottom edges of cover.

Things You Need:
- loose pages, all same size, for your book
- thicker paper, or cardboard
- blank paper
- 1 single-hole punch
- twine
- 1 ruler
- colored tape
- scissors

100 The World Book Student Discovery Encyclopedia

The World Book Student Discovery Encyclopedia 101

Activities Many activities are found in *Student Discovery*. These activities extend or enrich the subject of the article they accompany. For example, the **Book** article has instructions for a book-binding activity.

● How to use *Student Discovery*

Country articles Articles on countries and other selected political units are bordered in green and feature flags, maps, and fact boxes.

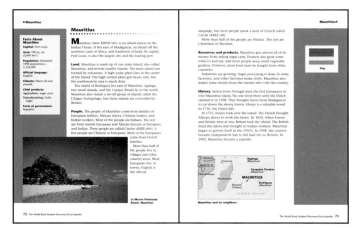

State articles Articles on U.S. states are bordered in blue and feature illustrations of the state flag, seal, bird, and flower. Also included are an outline map, a locator map, a fact box, and a list of important dates in the state's history.

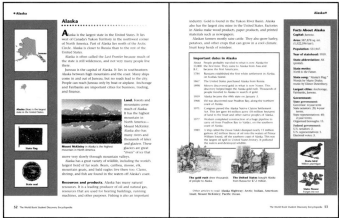

Province articles Articles on Canadian provinces are bordered in red and feature illustrations of the provincial flag, seal, and floral emblem. Also included are an outline map, a locator map, a fact box, and a list of important dates in the province's history.

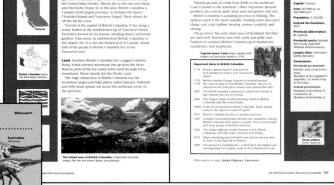

Special features Special feature articles give more detailed information and more illustrations on key subjects. The colored background used for these feature articles makes them easy to find.

Ii

is the ninth letter of the English alphabet.

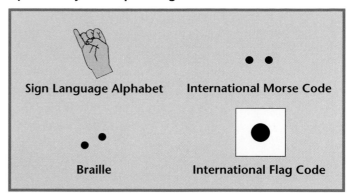

Sign Language Alphabet

International Morse Code

Braille

International Flag Code

Development of the letter I

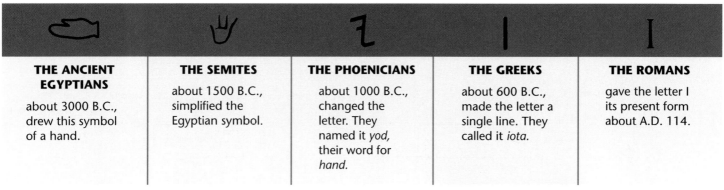

THE ANCIENT EGYPTIANS
about 3000 B.C., drew this symbol of a hand.

THE SEMITES
about 1500 B.C., simplified the Egyptian symbol.

THE PHOENICIANS
about 1000 B.C., changed the letter. They named it *yod,* their word for *hand.*

THE GREEKS
about 600 B.C., made the letter a single line. They called it *iota.*

THE ROMANS
gave the letter I its present form about A.D. 114.

Ice

Ice is frozen water. In nature, ice forms on lakes and rivers. It also forms on wet streets and sidewalks when the weather is cold. Snow, sleet, frost, and hail are other kinds of natural ice. Glaciers (*GLAY shuhrz*) are huge sheets of ice that cover large areas of land.

People use ice for many reasons. Millions of people use ice to chill drinks. The food industry ships and stores meat, fish, vegetables, and fruit in ice. The low temperature of ice slows the growth of germs that spoil food. People also treat burns or cuts with ice because it stops the growth of germs that could cause infection. Ice also helps stop bleeding and swelling.

Ice forms when the temperature of water falls to 32 °F (0 °C). This temperature is called the freezing point of water. Ice begins to melt when its surroundings become warmer than 32 °F.

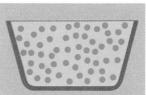

At room temperature, water molecules move about freely.

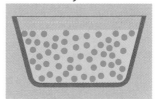

As water gets colder, the molecules move closer together.

When water freezes, the molecules move apart and form stiff crystals. The water becomes ice.

Ice is formed as water becomes colder and its molecules move closer together. When water freezes into ice, it expands and the molecules push apart.

People have used ice for thousands of years. Before ice machines were developed, people shipped ice from cold places to warm places. During the early 1800's, fast-moving ships carried ice from the northern United States to South America, India, and other warm places.

In 1851, John Gorrie, a surgeon from Florida, built the first commercial ice-making machine in the United States. He used the ice to cool his patients' rooms.

Other articles to read: **Frost; Glacier; Hail; Iceberg; Refrigerator.**

Ice Age

An ice age is a time in Earth's history when huge sheets of ice covered large areas of land. An ice age usually lasts about 100,000 years. The most recent ice age ended about 11,500 years ago. Most scientists believe there will be another ice age in the future.

The last ice age took place during a period of time called the Pleistocene Epoch (*PLY stuh SEEN EHP uhk*). This epoch took place from about 2 million years ago to about 11,500 years ago.

During this last ice age, large ice sheets called glaciers (*GLAY shuhrz*) formed in North America, Europe, and Asia. These sheets of ice slid slowly across the land. Prehistoric people and animals moved ahead of the ice to find food and places to live.

Some prehistoric people called Neanderthals (*nee AN duhr THAWLZ*) lived in what is now Europe during the last ice age. Many lived in caves to escape the harsh cold.

Huge mammoths and woolly rhinoceroses also roamed the frozen land. Their thick, shaggy coats helped them stay warm.

Woolly rhinoceroses roamed the land during the last ice age.

When the ice melted, the environment of many prehistoric people changed. This change greatly affected their way of life. In some places, people began to learn how to raise food. They became the first farmers.

Other articles to read: **Glacier.**

Ice cream

● ●

Ice cream is a popular frozen food. It is made mostly of milk, sugar, and flavorings. Ice cream comes in many flavors. The most popular flavor in the United States is vanilla.

People in many parts of the world eat ice cream. Most of the ice cream we eat today is made in ice cream factories.

Ice cream is eaten in many parts of the world.

Cool Ice Cream Cookiewiches

Things You Need:
- sugar cookies
- chocolate chip cookies
- paper cupcake holders (be sure the cookies will fit into the cupcake holders)
- ice cream—your favorite flavors
- spoon
- cookie sheet

Having a party? Try serving the coolest treat around: ice cream cookiewiches.

First, mix and match pairs of cookies! Put two cookies in each cupcake holder. Make enough to fill a cookie sheet.

Take the ice cream out of the freezer, uncover, and let it thaw for about five minutes. With a spoon, spread the ice cream on each bottom cookie, and top each with another cookie. Use different flavors of ice cream. Put the cookiewiches in the freezer until you are ready to serve them. Or, you can keep them in the refrigerator until about ten minutes before serving.

Ask your friends to try more than one cookiewich. Ask them which flavor of ice cream made the best cookiewich.

Wrap any extras in plastic wrap, and keep them in a covered container in the freezer. Your cookiewiches are now snackwiches. You can enjoy one anytime.

In an ice cream factory, milk and sugar are blended in a huge vat. Then the mixture is pasteurized (*PAS chuh ryzd*) to kill harmful germs. Next, it is homogenized (*huh MAWJ un nyzd*) to make the ice cream smooth. The mixture is then cooled. After flavorings and colorings are added, the mixture is put in a freezer. Fanlike blades in the freezer whip air bubbles into the ice cream. Without the air bubbles, ice cream would be as hard as ice cubes.

Then the ice cream is packaged. It is placed in a hardening room for at least 12 hours. Now it is ready to be shipped to stores.

Some people enjoy making their own ice cream. Homemade ice cream is not as smooth as the ice cream sold in stores. That's because it has been stirred by less powerful blades.

Jacob Fussell, an American milk dealer, started the first ice cream plant in Baltimore, Maryland, in 1851. Ice cream cones were first served at the 1904 World's Fair in St. Louis, Missouri. Ice cream bars appeared in 1921.

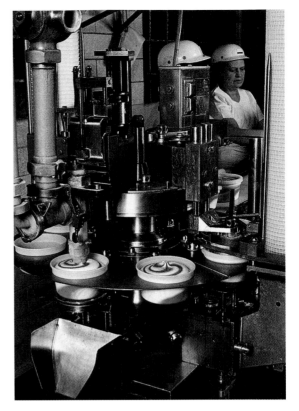

Most ice cream is made in factories.

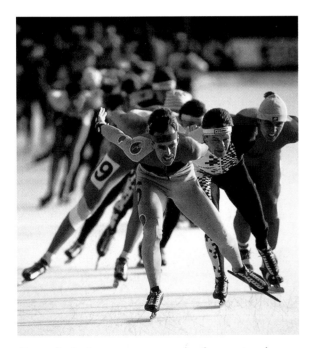

Speed skaters race around a frozen track.

Ice skating

Ice skating is a fun activity in which people glide over smooth ice on skates. The skates used in ice skating are boots with metal blades attached to the bottom. Many people enjoy skating outdoors on frozen ponds and rivers. Others like skating on indoor rinks where the ice is smoother. Also, on rinks, there is no danger of falling through thin ice. Ice skating is good exercise too.

Kinds of ice skating

There are two main ice-skating sports—figure skating and speed skating. Figure skaters perform leaps, spins, and other graceful movements. They usually skate to music. There are competitions for single skaters, for pairs (a man and a woman), and for ice dancing. The movements used in ice dancing are like the steps used in ballroom dancing.

In speed skating, the skaters race around a frozen track. They cover distances of 500 to 10,000 meters. Speed skaters swing their arms for a smooth, flowing motion. In races longer than 1,500 meters, they save energy by swinging only one arm.

In pack skating, a number of speed skaters take part in a series of races. The winners go on to the final races. Different races are held for children of different ages.

Many people enjoy watching figure skating and ice skating competitions. Champion figure skaters and trick skaters also thrill crowds at colorful ice shows. In addition, people enjoy playing or watching ice hockey, a fast sport in which players wear ice skates.

Skates

Figure-skating boots have higher tops than the boots worn by speed skaters. A figure-skate blade has two edges. Skaters skate on one edge at a time. The bottom of the blade curves slightly inward, so only a small part of it touches the ice at one time. This makes it easier to perform tricky movements. The front of the blade has several teeth, or jagged parts, that grip the ice during jumps and spins.

A speed-skate blade is straight, flat, and thin. These blades help the skater to start quickly and travel fast. Some skaters reach a speed of 35 miles (56 kilometers) per hour.

A hockey-skate blade is curved at each end. These curves enable the player to make turns and other moves more easily.

History of ice skating

People have skated on ice for at least 2,000 years. Remains of ice skates dating from 50 B.C. have been found in Roman ruins in London. The earliest skates were made of animal bones, which people

Types of ice skates

Figure skate
Hooks
Eyelets
Boot
Blade

Speed skate

Hockey skate

Figure skaters learn to perform graceful movements on the ice. These drawings show how to do an "axel" jump.

strapped onto boots. People used these skates to get around in winter. In time, they began to enjoy races too.

Skate blades made of iron were used in the Netherlands about 1250. All-steel blades were first made in the 1850's, and skating became popular. About 1870, an American ballet dancer named Jackson Haines started modern figure skating. Today, figure skating and speed skating are events in the Olympic Games.

Other articles to read: **Hockey, ice; Olympic Games.**

Iceberg

An iceberg is a huge piece of ice that floats in the sea. Some icebergs are many miles long. They are always bigger than they look. Most of the iceberg is under water.

Icebergs in the North Atlantic Ocean come from Greenland. They break off the ice sheet that covers Greenland and fall into the sea. Icebergs also come from the Antarctic icecap. Some of these icebergs are many times larger than those found in the North Atlantic. When an iceberg starts to break away, it makes noises that can be heard for miles. It sounds like loud explosions and rolling thunder. When it drops into the sea, it causes huge waves.

Icebergs can be dangerous to ships. The famous ship *Titanic* struck an iceberg and sank in 1912. About 1,500 people died.

Other articles to read: **Glacier.**

Iceberg

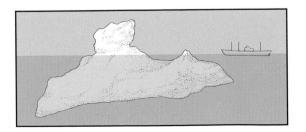

The top of an iceberg melts, leaving the bottom underwater. The hidden ice is dangerous to ships.

Iceland

● ●

Iceland is an island country in the North Atlantic Ocean, close to the Arctic Circle. Iceland is warmer than most places so far north because the Gulf Stream flows around it. The Gulf Stream is an ocean current that carries warm water from the south into parts of the North Atlantic.

Iceland is sometimes called the *Land of Ice and Fire*. Glaciers (*GLAY shuhrz*), or huge rivers of ice that flow very slowly, move past hot springs and volcanoes. Sometimes volcanoes erupt under the sea. A famous hot spring called Geysir spouts water about 195 feet (59 meters) into the air. Icelanders use water from hot springs to heat their buildings.

Most Icelanders live in villages and small towns near the coast. About half the people live in or around Reykjavik, the capital and largest city. Icelanders do not have family names. They have a first name, such as Erik or Inga. Their second name is made up of their father's first name followed by either *son* (for boys) or *dóttir* (for girls). If Erik and Inga's father's name was Jon, their names would be Erik Jonsson and Inga Jonsdóttir.

It is hard to grow crops on most of this windswept island. Small farms raise sheep, cattle, and small Icelandic horses. The sea is rich in fish, however. Many people catch fish or work in fish-freezing plants. Publishing, or making books and other things to read, is a major business in Iceland.

People from Scandinavia and Viking settlements in Britain settled in Iceland from about A.D. 870. They set up a meeting of leaders called the Althing, the world's oldest parliament. Iceland was ruled by Denmark from 1380 to 1944, when the people voted for independence. Today, the Althing is made up of elected lawmakers.

Other articles to read: **Viking**.

Iceland and its neighbors

Facts About Iceland

Capital: Reykjavik.

Area: 39,769 sq. mi. (103,000 km²).

Population: Estimated 1998 population—277,000.

Official language: Icelandic.

Climate: Mild summers and cool winters in the coastal lowlands; colder inland.

Chief products:
Agriculture: cattle, hay, market gardening, sheep.
Fishing: capelin, cod, haddock, herring.
Manufacturing and processing: aluminum, cement, clothing, electrical equipment, fertilizer, food processing, printing and bookbinding.

Form of government: Republic.

Flag

★ Boise

Idaho (blue) ranks 13th in size among the states.

State flag

State seal

Idaho

● ●

Idaho is a state in the Rocky Mountain region of the United States. Washington and Oregon border Idaho on the west. Montana and Wyoming lie to the east. Canada lies to the north. Nevada and Utah are south.

The capital and largest city of Idaho is Boise (*BOY zee*). It lies in the southwestern part of the state at the foot of the Boise Front Mountains. The Boise River flows through the city. Pocatello, Idaho's second largest city, is in the middle of a farming area. It serves as an important trading and shipping center for crops and livestock.

Land. Idaho is a land of awesome scenic wonders. It has snow-covered mountains, powerful river rapids, quiet lakes, steep canyons, and ice caves. The waters of the Snake River rush through Hells Canyon. Hells Canyon is even deeper than the Grand Canyon. Coeur d'Alene Lake is one of the most beautiful mountain lakes in the world. Shoshone Falls, on the Snake River, is higher than Niagara Falls.

The Rocky Mountains cover northern and central Idaho. Borah Peak, in the center of the state, is the highest mountain. Flatter land and many valleys lie among the mountains, where farmers raise wheat and peas. There are also peaceful lakes and colorful meadows. Herds of sheep graze on the mountain slopes during the summer.

The Columbia Plateau (*pla TOH*) sweeps across the lower part of the state. A plateau is an area of high, flat land. Part of the plateau is a large plain with farmland for crops and livestock.

Resources and products. Farming is important in Idaho. The biggest crop is potatoes. Idaho farmers also

Majestic mountains and beautiful lakes, rivers, and forests make Idaho one of the most scenic states.

grow wheat, hay, barley, and sugar beets. Many farmers raise cattle and run dairy farms.

In recent years, a number of small industries have moved to Idaho. Many factories now make computer parts, food products, machinery, and chemicals. Lumber and wood products are important too.

Silver and gold are mined in the mountains. Other important minerals include clays, copper, and crushed stone.

Important dates in Idaho

Indian days	Indian peoples that lived in the Idaho region before Europeans days arrived included the Nez Percé and the Shoshone.
1805	U.S. explorers Meriwether Lewis and William Clark passed through the Idaho region on their way to the Pacific Coast.
1809	David Thompson built the first fur-trading post in Idaho.
1860	Franklin, Idaho's first permanent settlement, was founded. Gold was discovered on Orofino Creek.
1863	The U.S. government established the Idaho Territory.
1874	Utah Northern Railroad entered Idaho Territory at Franklin.
1877	U.S. troops defeated the Nez Percé Indians in October in the Nez Percé War.
1890	Idaho became the 43rd U.S. state on July 3.
1951	For the first time in history, scientists used nuclear energy to create electricity. This feat was accomplished at the National Reactor Testing Station near Idaho Falls.
1955	Arco became the first community in the world to receive all of its power from nuclear energy. The National Reactor Testing Station supplied the town's power for one hour on July 17.
1972	Ninety-one miners died in a fire at the Sunshine silver mine in Shoshone County.
1990	Idaho celebrated its centennial (100th anniversary) as a state.

Explorers Lewis and Clark reached Idaho in 1805.

Chief Joseph and the Nez Percé Indians defeated U.S. troops at White Bird Canyon in June 1877.

Facts About Idaho

Capital: Boise.

Area: 83,574 sq. mi. (216,456 km²).

Population: 1,011,986.

Year of statehood: 1890.

State abbreviations: Ida. (traditional), ID (postal).

State motto: *Esto Perpetua* (Let It Be Perpetual).

State song: "Here We Have Idaho." Words by McKinley Helm and Albert J. Tompkins; music by Sallie Hume-Douglas.

Largest cities: Boise, Pocatello, Idaho Falls.

Government:
State government:
Governor: 4-year term.
State senators: 35; 2-year terms.
State representatives: 70; 2-year terms.
Counties: 44.

Federal government:
U.S. senators: 2.
U.S. representatives: 2.
Electoral votes: 4.

State bird
Mountain bluebird

State flower
Syringa

Illinois

● ●

Springfield
★

Illinois (blue) ranks 24th
in size among the states.

State flag

State seal

Illinois is a state in the Midwestern region of the United States. Iowa and Missouri lie to the west of Illinois. Indiana and Kentucky lie to the east and south. Wisconsin is north of Illinois. The northeast tip of Illinois borders Lake Michigan.

Illinois is also called the *Land of Lincoln*. Abraham Lincoln, the 16th president of the United States, spent most of his life in Illinois.

The historic city of Galena was home to President Grant.

Springfield, the capital of Illinois, lies in the middle of the state in a busy farming region. Abraham Lincoln's home still stands near the center of Springfield.

Chicago is the largest city in Illinois. It is a huge city along the shores of Lake Michigan. Millions of people live there. Chicago has interesting places to visit, such as museums and zoos. Its lakefront has beaches and colorful harbors.

Land. Most of Illinois is a gently rolling plain. Millions of years ago, glaciers—huge sheets of ice—moved very slowly across this land. The glaciers flattened the land and made small hills. Later, the region was covered with prairie grass. As the grass died out and rotted away, it made the soil very rich for farming.

Northwestern Illinois had no glaciers, so it has bigger hills and valleys. The Mississippi River forms the western border.

Resources and products. Illinois is one of the most important farming states in the country. Ever since pioneer days, corn has been the state's most important crop. Soybeans are second. Hay, wheat, rye, and oats are grown, too. Farmers also grow asparagus, cabbage, beans, and fruits.

Livestock production is a big business in Illinois, and there are many hog farms. Farmers also raise cattle and chickens.

Illinois is one of the leading coal-producing states. About two-thirds of Illinois sits on top of a huge coal bed.

The Chicago area is the second largest manufacturing region

in the United States. But factories all around the state make products such as food products, machinery, chemicals, metal products, printed materials, and computer products.

Important dates in Illinois

Indian days — Indian peoples known as mound builders lived in the Illinois region hundreds of years before Europeans arrived. They built huge mounds to bury their dead and to support temples. Monk's Mound, near Cahokia, is the largest such mound in the United States.

1673 — Louis Jolliet of Canada and Jacques Marquette of France explored parts of what is now Illinois.

1699 — French priests founded a settlement in Cahokia, the oldest town in Illinois.

1717 — The Illinois region became part of the French colony of Louisiana.

1763 — Great Britain took over what is now Illinois from France.

1778 — Virginia soldier George Rogers Clark and his forces captured Cahokia and Kaskaskia during the Revolutionary War.

1783 — The Illinois region became part of the United States under the treaty ending the Revolutionary War.

1818 — Illinois became the 21st state on December 3.

1832 — Illinois settlers defeated the Sauk and Fox Indians in the Black Hawk War.

1861 — Springfield lawyer Abraham Lincoln became the 16th president of the United States. He led the country through the Civil War (1861-1865).

1871 — The Chicago Fire destroyed much of the city.

1893 — The World's Columbian Exposition, an important international fair, was held in Chicago.

1920's — Illinois built many hard-surfaced roads for cars and trucks.

1942 — Scientists at the University of Chicago controlled an atomic chain reaction for the first time. This important event led to the development of the atomic bomb and of nuclear energy.

1986 — James R. Thompson became the first Illinois governor to be elected to a fourth term.

Other articles to read: **Black Hawk; Chicago; Grant, Ulysses S.; Jolliet, Louis; Lincoln, Abraham; Marquette, Jacques; Mississippi River; Mound builders; Reagan, Ronald; Wright, Frank Lloyd.**

The Lincoln-Douglas debates of 1858 were held in seven Illinois towns.

Facts About Illinois

Capital: Springfield.

Area: 56,343 sq. mi. (145,928 km²).

Population: 11,466,682.

Year of statehood: 1818.

State abbreviations: Ill. (traditional), IL (postal).

State motto: *State Sovereignty, National Union.*

State song: "Illinois." Words by Charles H. Chamberlin; sung to the tune of "Baby Mine" by Archibald Johnston.

Largest cities: Chicago, Rockford, Peoria, Springfield.

Government:
State government:
Governor: 4-year term.
State senators: 59; 2- or 4-year terms.
State representatives: 118; 2-year terms.
Counties: 102.

Federal government:
U.S. senators: 2.
U.S. representatives: 20.
Electoral votes: 22.

State bird Cardinal

State flower Native violet

Imagination

These children are using their imaginations to create special Mother's Day cards.

Imagination is the picturing of somthing in the mind. For example, it's a hot day. You daydream that you are swimming in a cool stream, or eating an ice cream cone. Neither the stream nor the ice cream cone are really there, of course. They are in your imagination.

When you imagine something, you think of it so clearly that you can sometimes make a picture of it in your mind. Imagination allows people to remember things they have seen and done before, and also to make up things they have never seen and never done.

A person who writes a story, paints a picture, or composes music is using his or her imagination. An inventor uses imagination to make something new from what is already known.

Other articles to read: **Dream.**

Immigration

Immigration means coming to another country to live. People who do this are immigrants in their new country. People who leave their own country to settle in another country are called emigrants.

Throughout history, millions of people have become immigrants. Often they faced dangers and hardships, trying to make a fresh start in a land where everything was new to them. The greatest immigration worldwide took place from the early 1800's to the 1930's. Most of these people came from Europe. More than half went to the United States.

Immigrants are people who come to a new country to live. A worker checks the papers of these immigrants as they arrive.

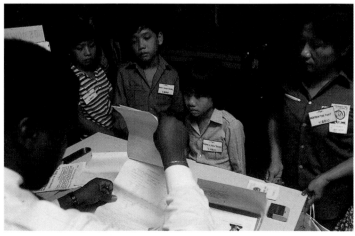

Immigration to the American colonies began in the 1600's. These were the Thirteen Colonies that later became the United States. The largest number of immigrants arrived between the 1880's and the early 1920's. Most of these people came from Europe. Today, most new immigrants come to the United States from Mexico, the Philippines and other parts of Asia, and the Caribbean.

Countries around the world have received large numbers of immigrants at certain times. For example, Jewish immigrants poured into the new nation of Israel soon after it was founded in 1948.

Some people have to flee from their own countries because of war or ill-treatment. Sometimes they have to leave to get enough to eat. These people are called refugees. But the main reason for immigration has been the chance to have a better job or better land for farming.

Immigrants take an oath to become citizens of their new country.

Immune system

● ●

The immune system protects the body from sickness. It often fights off some illnesses before people know they are sick. Even when people feel ill, their immune system is working hard to stop the illness before it causes much harm. Sometimes doctors give people medicine that helps the immune system fight an illness.

Many parts of the body work together in the immune system. Some of the most important parts are white blood cells. White blood cells are round and colorless. They are so tiny that they can be seen only with a microscope.

White blood cells are one of the body's strongest weapons against things that cause illness. These things include *bacteria* and *viruses*.

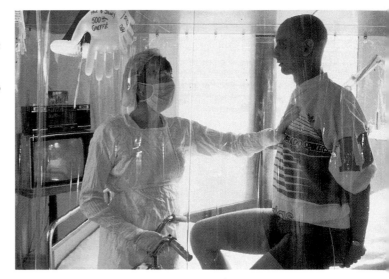

If a person's immune system isn't working properly, special care must be taken to protect against disease.

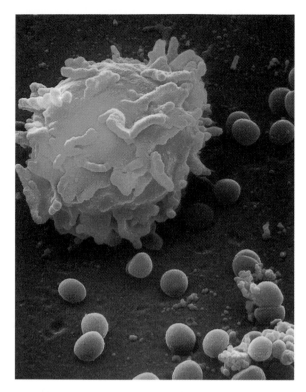

This white blood cell surrounded by yellow bacteria cells can only be seen through a microscope.

Immunizations help protect people and animals from disease.

Bacteria and viruses are tiny "invaders," seen only with a microscope, that enter the body. They can cause colds, sore throats, upset stomachs, and many other such illnesses. Some white blood cells surround bacteria and digest them. Other white blood cells produce substances that kill bacteria and viruses or make them harmless. These substances are called antibodies.

Sometimes the immune system makes mistakes. It tries to protect the body from substances that do not cause illness. These substances may be things like pollen, which is the harmless dust that comes from plants, dust, mold, and feathers. When the immune system acts as though these things are harmful, it causes an *allergy.* A person with an allergy to a certain substance may sneeze or get itchy because of it.

Other articles to read: **AIDS; Allergy; Disease; Immunization; Inoculation**

Immunization

● ●

Immunization (*IHM yuh nyz ay shuhn*) is a way of protecting the body against a disease. The body can fight many diseases by producing substances called antibodies. One type of immunization causes the body to make antibodies against a disease without actually causing the disease. This type of immunization is called vaccination (*vak sihn NAY shuhn*). Another type of immunization uses a *serum,* which has antibodies already in it.

A British doctor named Edward Jenner made the first vaccine (*vak SEEN*) in 1796. He used it to prevent a disease called smallpox. Today, we have vaccines to prevent measles, mumps, whooping cough, and many other diseases. Most vaccines are given as shots. But some are swallowed.

Other articles to read: **Disease; Immune system; Inoculation; Pasteur, Louis; Salk, Jonas Edward**

Impressionism

● ●

Impressionism (*ihm PRESH uh nihz uhm*) is a style of art. Impressionism became popular in France in the late 1800's. The French impressionists often worked outdoors and painted quickly. The impressionists studied the science of color and light. They wanted to catch the way light changed the look of an object. The artist Claude Monet, for example, painted a haystack at different times of the day. Each painting was different because the sunlight hit the haystack in a different way.

Impressionists also created music, writings, and sculpture, using sounds, words, and shapes to make people think of certain images or ideas.

Other articles to read: **Cassatt, Mary; Degas, Edgar; Monet, Claude; Renoir, Pierre Auguste; Van Gogh, Vincent.**

This impressionist painting by Renoir shows the effect of sunlight on figures and flowers.

Inca

● ●

The Inca (*IHNG kuh*) were a South American Indian people. They ruled one of the largest and richest empires in North and South America. The Inca took over the lands of their neighbors and governed well. They built roads, bridges, and stone temples. They learned how to water desert land and cut huge flat steps into hillsides to grow crops. Their empire lasted from about 1438 to the 1530's. Spanish soldiers, who came in 1532, fought the Inca and destroyed their empire.

An Inca emperor is shown entering the Temple of the Sun in Cusco. The mummy of a former emperor is seated nearby (*left*).

Gold objects like these figures of a man and a llama were used by families of Inca nobles.

Descendants of the Inca live today the way their ancestors did.

Daily life

Most Inca were farmers. They grew corn, cotton, and potatoes. They also grew and ate a root called oca and a grain called quinoa. The Inca made clothing from wool and cotton. Men wore tunics, with a cloak for cold weather. Women wore long dresses and shawls. Rich people wore fine clothing and jewelry.

Most people lived in mud and stone houses with straw roofs. Nobles, or rich and important people, lived in large palaces and had fine pottery and gold objects. The palaces were built of huge stones fitted together without cement.

The Inca had no writing and no money system. Instead, they traded and exchanged products. They sent messages by runners. They also used fires and smoke signals. The Inca used knotted strings to keep records. They had no wheels, so most people walked. Nobles were carried in a litter, a wooden frame with a couch. Servants carried the litter on their shoulders. Llamas carried all the heavy loads.

Inca beliefs

Religion was important to the Inca. Their chief god was Viracocha. The emperor also prayed to the sun god Inti. Inca people never made a decision without trying to find out the will of the gods.

Rise and fall of the Inca

The Inca homeland was around Cusco in what is now southern Peru. Around the year 1200, the Inca began to spread out and rule over their neighbors.

The Inca empire began about 1438 when the ruler Pachacuti made Cusco the center of government. The Inca empire grew to include parts of what are now Colombia, Ecuador, Peru, Bolivia, Chile, and Argentina.

Pachacuti's grandson, Huayna Capac, died about 1527. Two of his sons, Huáscar and Atahualpa, fought one another over control of the empire. In 1532, Atahualpa won. But that same year a Spanish force of 167 men led by Francisco Pizarro marched into Peru. The Spaniards defeated the Inca and captured Atahualpa. They demanded a room filled with gold and a room filled twice with silver for his freedom. The Inca gave them this treasure, but the Spaniards killed Atahualpa anyway.

Huáscar was already dead. He had been killed on Atahualpa's orders. So now the Inca had no leader. The Inca could not stop the Spaniards from taking over their empire. The Spaniards tried to wipe out all the Inca customs, but they failed. Today, some Indians in Peru and some other countries still live much as the Inca did. They speak Quechua, the Inca language. They weave cloth in the Inca style, and they practice Inca healing ceremonies.

Other articles to read: **Peru.**

Independence Day

● ●

Independence Day in the United States of America is celebrated on July 4 each year to celebrate the country's birthday. On July 4, 1776, the Declaration of Independence was adopted by a group of American leaders called the Continental Congress. Independence Day has been celebrated on July 4 ever since. In 1941, the U.S. Congress made July 4 a national holiday.

In the early days, fireworks and gunfire were part of Independence Day celebrations. However, many people were hurt or killed in accidents, so many cities and states made the sale of fireworks against the law in the 1900's. People today mark Independence Day with parades and programs, games and plays, athletic contests, and picnics. Some cities hire people trained to put on a fireworks display. Americans everywhere join in the national celebration.

Other articles to read: **Declaration of Independence.**

A huge American flag is part of this Independence Day parade in Atlanta, Georgia.

Flag

India

India is a large country in southern Asia. It has more people than any other country in the world except China.

India is bordered by Pakistan and the Arabian Sea in the west. China, Nepal, and Bhutan lie on the north. To the east are Bangladesh, Myanmar, and the Bay of Bengal. The Indian Ocean lies to the south.

The capital of India is New Delhi in northern India. New Delhi was built in the early 1900's. It is a modern city with skyscrapers and wide, tree-lined streets. The city has many gardens, parks, and fountains too.

Mumbai, which used to be called Bombay, is India's largest city. It is also the country's chief western seaport. Mumbai lies on an island off western India. Bridges link the city with the mainland of India.

Land. The northern half of India is made up of the Himalaya region and the Northern Plains.

The Himalaya region stretches across northeast India. The Himalaya are the highest mountains in the world.

India is one of the most crowded countries in the world. Cities like Bangalore *above* are busy.

Snow covers the tallest peaks the year around. Tigers, deer, and rhinoceroses roam the lower slopes.

South of the Himalaya region lie the Northern Plains. This is a low, flat area with wide valleys made by the Brahmaputra, Indus, and Ganges rivers. India's richest farmland is found in these river valleys. The Thar Desert lies in the western part of the Northern Plains.

The Ganges River is India's greatest river. It starts high in the Himalaya and flows into the Bay of Bengal.

The southern half of India is a peninsula that juts into the Indian Ocean. A peninsula is land that has water on three sides. The Deccan Plateau (*pla TOH*) forms most of India's southern peninsula. Mountains called the Eastern Ghats rise along the east coast. The Western Ghats stretch along the west coast. Elephants, monkeys, and other wildlife roam in the forests of the mountains.

People. India has many different groups of people. The two largest are the Dravidians (*drah VIH dee uhnz*) and the Indo-Aryans (*ihn doh AHR yuhnz*). Most Dravidians live in the south. Most Indo-Aryans live in the north. Smaller groups live in the country's forest and hill areas.

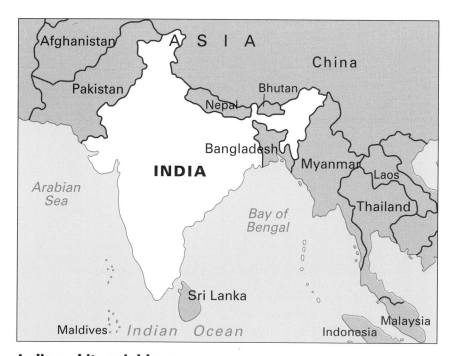

India and its neighbors

Facts About India

Capital: New Delhi.

Area: 1,269,346 sq. mi. (3,287,590 km²).

Population: Estimated 1998 population— 986,026,000.

Official languages: Hindi, English, Sanskrit, and 16 local languages.

Climate: Mild and cool from October to February, and hot from March to June in northern India. The south stays hot all year round. From June to September, rain is brought by seasonal winds called monsoons.

Chief products:

Agriculture: bananas, beans, chickpeas, coconuts, cotton, jute, mangoes, onions, oranges, peanuts, pepper, potatoes, rice, sesame seeds, sorghum, sugar cane, tea, wheat.

Manufacturing and processing: bicycles, brassware and silverware, cement, chemicals, cloth and clothing, fertilizer, food products, iron and steel, jute bags and rope, leather goods, machinery, medicines, motor vehicles, paper, petroleum products, rugs, sewing machines, sugar, wood products.

Mining: coal, iron ore, limestone, petroleum.

Form of government: Federal republic.

Most people in India live in villages and farm the nearby fields.

More than 1,000 languages are spoken in India. Almost half the people speak Hindi, India's national language. Most of India's people live in villages and farm the nearby fields. These farmers often live in small houses made of dried mud and straw.

In recent years, many country people have moved to the cities to look for work. As a result, the cities are now overcrowded. There aren't enough homes, water, or electric power for all the people. Many people live on the streets or in one-room shacks.

Religion is important to the Indian people. Most are Hindus, but there are some Muslims, Buddhists, Christians, Jains, and Sikhs.

Resources and products. Most people in India are farmers. They grow crops mainly to feed their families. Rice is the biggest crop, but they grow wheat, corn, and many other crops, too.

India is the world's leading producer of many plant products. These include cauliflower, mangoes, sesame seeds, and tea.

India has more cattle than any other country. In most of India, farmers use cattle to plow the land. Dairy farming is also important. Farmers sell milk from their water buffaloes and use animal skins to make leather goods.

India is one of the world's top producers of iron and steel. Indian factories use the iron and steel to make airplanes, cars, bicycles, and other products. India has many cotton mills too.

Many Indians make handcrafted items at home or in small factories. These include carpets, brass objects, jewelry, leather goods, and wood carvings.

India is rich in iron ore, coal, and petroleum. The country has smaller deposits of many other minerals. It also has deposits of diamonds, emeralds, gold, and silver.

History. India is an ancient land. About 4,500 years ago, a group of people in the Indus River Valley built cities. They had ways of writing, counting, measuring, and weighing things. About 3,700 years ago, the Indus Valley people died out, but no one knows why.

About 3,500 years ago, Aryan people from central Asia settled in northern India. When they arrived, they found a people called the Dravidians. The warlike Aryans took over the Dravidians' land and pushed some of them south. The Aryans built villages and developed the Hindu religion.

For hundreds of years, India was controlled by a series of dynasties (*DY nuh steez*), or ruling families. One of these dynasties was founded by Babur, a Muslim, in 1526. When this dynasty ruled India, it was known as the Mughal Empire. In 1498, Vasco de Gama, a Portuguese explorer, reached India. The Portuguese took over areas on the western coast.

During the 1600's, the British became very powerful in India. In the 1700's and 1800's they expanded their control over most of India. In 1857, the Indian people rebelled against the British. But the British quickly stopped the rebellion.

In the late 1800's and early 1900's, more Indians began speaking out against British rule. By 1920, Mohandas K. Gandhi was a leader in the struggle for the independence of India. During this time, there was much fighting between India's Hindus and Muslims. The Muslims wanted their own country, and they wanted to call it Pakistan. In 1947, Indian and British leaders divided India into two independent nations—India and Pakistan.

Other articles to read: **Buddhism; Calcutta; Gandhi, Indira; Gandhi, Mohandas Karamchand; Ganges River; Himalaya; Hinduism; Islam; Muslims; New Delhi; Sikhism; Taj Mahal.**

Religion is important in India. This beautiful Jain temple is in Calcutta.

Indian, American

The American Indians were the first people to live in the Americas. They were living there for thousands of years before the Europeans arrived. Today, many Indians call themselves Native Americans. In Canada, they are called Aboriginal or native peoples.

The Indians probably came from Asia at least 15,000 years ago. At that time, there was a land area instead of water between Asia and North America. The Indians followed the animals they hunted across this land from Asia to what is now Alaska. The distance was about 50 miles (80 kilometers). Today, the land that connected the continents is covered by water. It is called the Bering Strait.

Over time, the Indians spread all across the Americas. When Christopher Columbus arrived in 1492, Indians were living from the Arctic in the north all the way to the tip of South America. Columbus thought he had reached the Indies, which then included India, China, the East Indies, and Japan. So he called the people he met "Indians."

Hundreds of Indian tribes with different ways of life lived in the Americas. The colored areas on the map show where tribes had similar lifestyles.

Cliff dwellers lived on the desert where Utah, Colorado, Arizona, and New Mexico come together.

Indian life before the Europeans

The Indians formed hundreds of groups, or tribes, across North and South America. Each tribe had their own way of life and their own language.

Different tribes of Indians lived all across North America. The Mohawk Indians hunted animals in the forest and grew crops for food.

Some tribes, such as the Aztec and the Maya of Central America, built large cities. The Indians of eastern North America and other tribes lived in small villages. Indians who lived at the tip of South America moved from place to place looking for food.

Indian families spent most of their time finding food, clothing, and a place to live. The families joined together in bands. Several bands in the same area formed tribes.

The food Indians ate depended on where they lived. Some hunted or fished for most of their food. Others got most of their food from gathering wild seeds, nuts, and roots. The Plains Indians of the central United States ate mostly buffalo meat and other game. The Pueblo Indians of the Southwest, the Middle American Indians who lived in Central America, and the Indians of the Andes were farmers. These tribes grew beans, corn, and squash.

Many Indians made their clothes from animal skins and fur. Some tribes of the Northwest Coast of North America made cloth from tree bark and plants called reeds. The Pueblo, Aztec, Inca, Maya, and some Caribbean tribes wove cotton cloth.

Indians built many kinds of homes. Some groups, such as the Haida of the Northwest Coast, built houses big enough for several families. In Canada, some Inuit (*IHN yoo iht*), who were once called Eskimos, built houses of snow in winter. They made tents of animal skins in the summer.

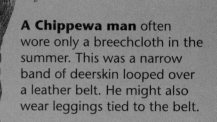

A Chippewa man often wore only a breechcloth in the summer. This was a narrow band of deerskin looped over a leather belt. He might also wear leggings tied to the belt.

The Tlingit Indians in the Northwest built houses of wood. In the chief's compartment, the cedarwood boards were painted with designs.

A Navajo woman teaches her daughter how to weave on a traditional loom. In this way, she helps to pass on part of Navajo culture to the next generation.

With horses, the Plains Indians could travel faster, carry heavier loads, and hunt and fight with greater skill.

The Pawnee dug large pits on the ground and covered them with layers of grassy earth called sod. They were called earth lodges. The Plains Indians built cone-shaped tepees of buffalo skins. The Indians of the Northeast made dome-shaped wigwams covered with leaves or bark.

The Indians did not have horses or cattle before the Europeans came. They traveled mostly by water. Many Indians made narrow boats, called canoes, of tree bark. They were light and easy to carry. They also made light boats from reeds. Most people carried their own loads. The Plains Indians used dogs (before horses) to pull their loads, too.

The arrival of the Europeans

Many European explorers and settlers came to the Americas in the 1500's and 1600's. Their arrival ended the Indian way of life forever.

Explorers, fur traders, and settlers spread across the New World. Missionaries, who wanted to teach the Indians about Christianity, also came to the New World. At first, most of the Indians did not mind the newcomers. They taught the settlers many things. European explorers followed Indian trails to find water and deposits of copper, gold, and other minerals. The Indians showed the settlers how to travel by canoe. They also taught the newcomers how to grow foods they had never seen before. These new crops included avocados, corn, peanuts, peppers, pineapples, potatoes, squash, and tomatoes.

The Europeans brought many things to the Indians. These included metal tools, guns, and liquor. They also brought cattle and horses.

The Indians and the Europeans had very different ways of life. Some Europeans tried to understand the Indians' ways. But others cheated the Indians and stole their land. When the Indians fought back, thousands of them were killed. Even more died from diseases the settlers brought from Europe. These diseases included measles and smallpox.

Land was a big problem between the Indians and the white settlers. The settlers wanted the land for farming, for grazing their cattle, and for mining. They believed they should own the land. But the Indians did not believe that anyone could own land. Instead, Indians saw themselves as caretakers of the land. So when the Indians signed over land to the white settlers, they thought that they could still hunt and farm the land too. But the settlers thought that the land belonged only to them. As a result, bitter fights broke out between the Indians and the settlers.

As the years went by, more settlers moved westward across North America. The Indians were forced off land that had been their home for centuries. Most Indians were made to move onto reservations. These reservations were large areas of land set aside by the U.S. government for the Indians.

Indians today

Most Indians in North America still do not completely follow the ways of white people. In some areas of Central and South America, several tribes have kept their language and their way of life. But most tribes have a new way of life that is a mixture of Indian and European customs.

Many Native Americans in the United States work hard to keep control of their land and their rights to fish and hunt. They would also like to handle Indian matters without the government getting involved. And they try to protect their land and waters from pollution.

Other articles to read: **Aztecs; Black Hawk; Brant, Joseph; Crazy Horse; French and Indian wars; Inca; Indian wars; Inuit; Joseph, Chief; Mound builders; Osceola; Pocahontas; Pontiac; Quanah; Sacagawea; Sand painting; Sequoyah; Sitting Bull; Tecumseh; Thorpe, Jim; Totem; Wigwam; Winnemucca, Sarah.**

Modern powwows feature Native American music and dancing. These gatherings bring tribes together to celebrate their heritage.

American Indian culture and heritage is preserved in some American museums. Displayed above is a cone-shaped tepee made from buffalo skin. The Plains Indians built this type of tepee.

Sign language helped different Indian tribes of the Plains talk together. Here are some sign language "words."

hungry　　dog　　tepee　　sleep　　drink

Indian Ocean

• •

The Indian Ocean is the third largest ocean in the world. It is almost totally surrounded by land—Africa, Asia, Australia, and Antarctica. Because of its smaller size and its position among large bodies of land, the Indian Ocean's tides are not as great as the tides of the Atlantic and Pacific oceans. Tides are the rise and fall of the ocean waters. The pull of the sun and the moon causes the tides.

Currents also move the ocean waters. Currents are like rivers in the ocean. The wind causes the currents in the Indian Ocean to move in a certain direction. Those in the northern part of the ocean move west in winter and east in summer. Those in the southern part of the ocean move in a circle.

Ships passing through the Suez Canal and Red Sea link Europe and Eastern Asia by way of the Indian Ocean. There are huge oil fields underneath the Indian Ocean. People use this oil for running machines and other purposes.

Other articles to read: **Suez Canal.**

The Indian Ocean

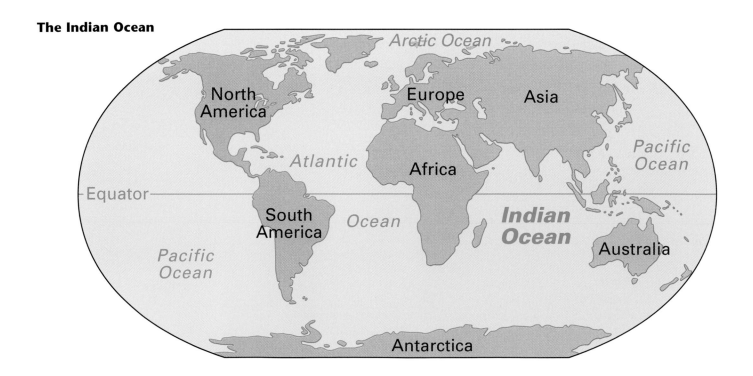

Indian wars

● ●

The Indian wars were the battles between American Indians and white people for the lands that became the United States.

English settlers started their first small colonies along the Atlantic coast of the United States in the early 1600's. At first, the colonists and the Indians got along well together. But soon more and more colonists began moving onto Indian lands. Disagreements grew into wars. The Indian wars lasted until the 1890's.

Most Indian wars started with a fight between an Indian tribe and the whites who lived nearby. Sometimes an Indian or a settler would be killed during the fight. This would start an Indian war. Sometimes other Indian tribes joined the fighting.

The Indians and white colonists got into wars mainly because they did not understand each other's way of life. The Indians hunted wild animals for food and clothing. The colonists were farmers, and they cut forests down to make farmland. Without the forests, the wild animals had nowhere to live. So the Indians either had to move on to new hunting grounds or stay and fight.

As time went on, more colonists came to settle the land. They had big families, and they wanted more land. They outnumbered the Indians and pushed them westward. In the end, the American Indians lost the battle for their land and their way of life.

Other articles to read: **Black Hawk; Boone, Daniel; Brant, Joseph; Colonies, Thirteen; Crazy Horse; Custer, George Armstrong; French and Indian Wars; Geronimo; Hiawatha; Joseph, Chief; Osceola; Pontiac; Sitting Bull; Smith, John; Tecumseh.**

Indian wars in America began in colonial times and lasted until the 1890's.

Indiana (blue) ranks 38th in size among the states.

State flag

State seal

Indiana

Indiana is a state in the Midwestern region of the United States. It lies between Illinois and Ohio. Michigan borders Indiana on the north, and Kentucky lies to the south. Lake Michigan lies at the northwestern tip of the state.

Indiana is called the *Hoosier State.* But no one knows for sure where the word *hoosier* came from.

Indianapolis, the capital and largest city of Indiana, lies in the middle of the state. It is sometimes called the *Crossroads of America.* Indianapolis is a major center for manufacturing and shipping. Indianapolis is also famous for automobile racing. The most important races are the Indianapolis 500 and the Brickyard 400.

Land. Much of Indiana is a low plain with rolling hills and shallow valleys. Millions of years ago, glaciers—giant sheets of ice—moved very slowly across this land. The glaciers flattened the land and made small hills. Later, the area was covered with prairie grass. As the grass died out and rotted away, it made the soil rich for farming.

Cataract Falls lies on the Eel River in Indiana. The state's natural beauty makes it a popular vacation place.

The south part of Indiana never had any glaciers, however. Instead, it has a series of steep hills called *knobs.* Some underground streams have made deep caves in the earth. Indiana also has miles of sand dunes in the north, along the shores of Lake Michigan.

The Wabash River and its branches are Indiana's most important rivers. Indiana also has many lakes and waterfalls.

Resources and products. Indiana is a major farming state. Farmers grow corn, soybeans, hay, and wheat. They also grow vegetables, such as tomatoes, cucumbers, onions, potatoes, and snap beans.

Livestock production is important too. Indiana farmers raise hogs, cattle, turkey, ducks, and sheep.

Indiana is a leading manufacturing state. Factories make car, truck, and airplane parts. They also make steel, aluminum, chemicals, and machinery. Indiana's mines produce coal, crushed stone, sand, and gravel.

Important dates in Indiana

Indian days	The first people to live in what is now Indiana were probably Native Americans known as mound builders. They buried their dead in large mounds, many of which can be seen today.
1679	French explorer Robert Caveliér, Sieur de La Salle, traveled into the Indiana region.
1732?	The French founded Vincennes, Indiana's first permanent settlement.
1763	France gave up the Indiana region to Great Britain after the French and Indian War.
1779	During the Revolutionary War in America, Virginia soldier George Rogers Clark and his troops captured Vincennes from the British. This victory gave the Americans control over the Indiana region.
1800	The U.S. government set up the Indiana Territory.
1811	General William Henry Harrison's troops defeated an army of several Indian tribes in the Battle of Tippecanoe.
1816	Indiana became the 19th U.S. state on December 11.
1894	Elwood Haynes designed one of the first successful gasoline-powered automobiles in Kokomo.
1911	The first Indianapolis 500 automobile race was held.
1956	Engineers completed the Northern Indiana Toll Road, a large highway.
1980's and 1990's	Indianapolis carried out building programs called redevelopment projects. New offices, hotels, and other buildings were built in older sections of the city.

Other articles to read: **Automobile racing; Harrison, William Henry; La Salle, Sieur de; Mound builders; Tecumseh.**

Tecumseh led the Indian tribes against the settlers until the Indians were defeated at the Battle of Tippecanoe in 1811.

Facts About Indiana

Capital: Indianapolis.

Area: 36,185 sq. mi. (93,720 km²).

Population: 5,564,228.

Year of statehood: 1816.

State abbreviations: Ind. (traditional), IN (postal).

State motto *The Crossroads of America.*

State song: "On the Banks of the Wabash, Far Away." Words and music by Paul Dresser.

Largest cities: Indianapolis, Fort Wayne, Evansville, Gary.

Government:
State government:
Governor: 4-year term.
State senators: 50; 4-year terms.
State representatives: 100; 2-year terms.
Counties: 92.

Federal government:
U.S. senators: 2.
U.S. representatives: 10.
Electoral votes: 12.

State bird
Cardinal

State flower
Peony

Flag

Indonesia

● ●

Indonesia is a country in Southeast Asia. It is made up of more than 13,500 islands. These islands stretch thousands of miles across the Pacific and Indian oceans between the rest of Asia and Australia. All the islands lie near the equator (*ih KWAY tuhr*). The equator is an imaginary line around the middle of the earth halfway between the North and South Poles.

Jakarta is the capital and largest city of Indonesia. It lies on the island of Java.

The islands. The islands of Indonesia are divided into three groups: the Greater Sunda Islands, the Lesser Sunda Islands, and the Moluccas. The western half of the island of New Guinea is also a province of Indonesia.

Most Indonesians live on one of the Greater Sunda Islands. These islands include Borneo, Sulawesi, Java, and Sumatra.

Borneo is the third-largest island in the world. A small part of it belongs to Brunei and Malaysia. A much larger part, called Kalimantan, belongs to Indonesia. Kalimantan has thick tropical rain forests and mountains.

Sulawesi, the most mountainous island of Indonesia, has many volcanoes. Java has more people than any of the other islands. In Sumatra, mountains cover part of the island, while farms, swamps, and thick rain forests cover other parts.

The Lesser Sunda Islands stretch from Bali to Timor. These islands have many mountains. The western islands of this region have more tropical rain forests than do the drier eastern islands.

The Moluccas lie between Sulawesi and New Guinea.

Indonesia and its neighbors

Rice is Indonesia's main food crop. These rice terraces are in Bali, Indonesia.

Halmaher is the largest island of this group. Hundreds of coral reefs and islands lie between the larger islands.

People. About 300 different groups of people live in Indonesia. The Javanese and Sudanese are the largest groups. The people of Indonesia speak more than 250 languages. Bahasa Indonesia is the official language. Most Indonesians follow the religion of Islam.

Most Indonesians live in small farm villages. Their main food is rice. They serve it with meat, fish, and vegetables. Village women often wear colorful skirts called sarongs. The men wear pants or sarongs.

Some farm families still live in traditional Indonesian houses that stand on stilts, or wooden poles, about 6 feet (1.8 meters) high. Some Indonesian people build long houses. About 100 people live in each long house.

Some Indonesians, especially in Java, have only one name. For example, the name of the country's first president was Sukarno.

Facts About Indonesia

Capital: Jakarta.

Area: 735,358 sq. mi. (1,904,569 km²).

Population: Estimated 1998 population— 206,491,000.

Official language: Bahasa Indonesia.

Climate: Hot and humid, with wet and dry seasons caused by major winds called monsoons.

Chief products:

Agriculture: bananas, cassava, cocoa, coconuts, coffee, corn, hogs, palm oil, poultry and eggs, rice, rubber, spices, sugar cane, sweet potatoes, tea, tobacco.

Fishing: shrimp, tuna.

Forest industry: plywood, rattan, teak, timber.

Manufacturing: cement, chemicals, cigarettes, cloth and clothing, fertilizers, footwear, petroleum, rubber products, steel, wood products.

Mining: bauxite, coal, copper, natural gas, nickel, petroleum, silver, tin.

Form of government: Republic.

Resources and products. Farming is the chief industry of Indonesia. Coffee, palm oil, rubber, sugar cane, tea, and tobacco are grown on big plantations. Rice, the most important food crop, is grown mostly on small farms.

Indonesia has large deposits of petroleum, natural gas, and tin. It is one of the chief producers of petroleum in the world. Petroleum and natural gas are used for heating homes, running machines, and other purposes.

Indonesia has a growing fishing industry. Large fleets catch anchovies, mackerel, sardines, scad, and tuna. Indonesia's forests produce valuable hardwoods, such as ebony and teak. Manufacturing is growing in Indonesia, too.

History. As early as 4,500 years ago, ancient Indonesians made tools of iron and bronze, wore cloth, and sailed the seas as traders. Later, small kingdoms developed on the islands, especially on Java and Sumatra.

In the 1200's, the Indonesian islands were part of a large trading route between Arabia and China. Portuguese, English, and Dutch traders arrived in the 1500's. They fought for control of the islands. By the late 1700's, the Dutch controlled most of the trading. The region became known as the Dutch East Indies or the Netherlands Indies.

In the early 1900's, the Indonesians began to speak out for independence. Sukarno was the leader of the independence movement. During World War II (1939-1945), Japanese forces took over Indonesia. After the war, the Dutch tried to take back the country, but there was much fighting between the Dutch and the Indonesians.

In 1949, Indonesia gained its independence. Sukarno became the nation's first president.

Other articles to read: **Jakarta.**

This traditional Legong Dance is performed in Ubud, Indonesia. About 300 different groups of people live in Indonesia.

Industrial Revolution

● ●

The Industrial Revolution was both a time period and a series of changes that took place in the way people lived and worked. These changes happened in the 1700's and early 1800's. During this time, people began to use certain kinds of machines to do work. These machines were powered by fuels such as steam or coal. Before the Industrial Revolution, people had done work by hand or with simple machines.

Women and children operated machines in factories during the Industrial Revolution.

The Industrial Revolution began in Great Britain during the 1700's. It spread to other parts of Europe and to North America beginning in the early 1800's.

Before the Industrial Revolution, most people worked at home on farms or in small village workshops. The workers supplied most of the power for making things. Water wheels made power too.

In the 1700's, people began wanting more products to buy. Traders began looking for ways to make things cheaply. At about the same time, the steam engine was invented. Spinning machines for making cloth were invented too. New ways to make iron were also found.

These new machines, and the workers to use them, were brought together for the first time in factories. Factories began to produce large amounts of goods for less money. The world soon changed from one that was made up of farms and villages where people worked at home to one where most people lived in cities and worked in factories.

Other articles to read: **Coal; Factory; Invention; Railroad.**

Railroads became important for carrying people and cargo during the 1830's. Horse-drawn and steam-powered trains like these were used in France in the mid-1800's.

Infant. See Baby.

Inflation

● ●

Inflation is a continuous increase in prices. If the cost of such things as food, houses, clothes, travel, and movies keeps going up, then there is inflation. In a time of inflation, prices go up and the value of money goes down. The value of money depends on what the money can buy. For example, suppose that a student could buy five pencils for a dollar last year. But this year the student can buy only four pencils for a dollar. The value of the dollar this year is less than it was last year. So the value of money has gone down.

Here is another example of inflation: Suppose a worker's pay goes up by $10 during a time when there is no inflation. The worker can then spend $10 more for things he or she wants, such as new shoes. But when there is inflation, prices go up. The worker cannot buy as many shoes as before.

Inflation can happen when people want things that they cannot find in the stores. People will then pay higher prices to get what they want. Inflation can also happen when workers get paid more money. Some businesses may raise prices in order to pay their workers more money.

Inflation affects people's lives. Some people may have to borrow money in order to pay for things that cost a lot. Some may start a garden to grow their own food in order to save money. The government sometimes helps control prices or workers' pay.

Inflation in Germany in the 1920's was so bad that prices were very high and money was almost worthless. People needed baskets of money just to buy food.

Influenza

Influenza (*ihn floo EHN zuh*) is a disease. It is often called flu (*floo*). People catch flu from other people. It is caused by a virus (*VY ruhs*), or germ. People with flu have chills, fever, and headaches. Their bodies ache, and they feel weak. Flu usually lasts about a week.

People with flu breathe the virus out into the air. Other people catch flu by breathing in the virus. It gets into the nose, throat, and lungs and may spread within the body.

People can get vaccinations (*VAK sih NAY shuhnz*), or shots, that protect them against flu. Many people get flu shots at the beginning of winter. More people catch flu in winter, maybe because they spend more time indoors together.

Other articles to read: **Immunization; Inoculation.**

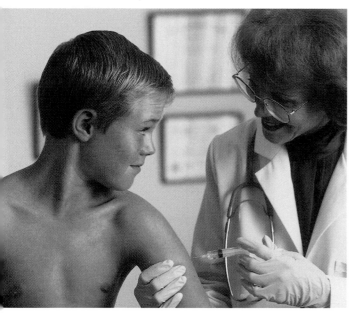

Vaccinations can protect people from flu.

In-line skating

In-line skating is a type of roller skating in which people glide along on wheeled boots called in-line skates. However, the wheels of the skates are placed in a different way from roller skates. In-line skates have four or five wheels set one behind the other. Roller skates have two pairs of wheels set side by side. In-line skating is a fun and active sport.

In-line skates have a high boot that covers the ankle. The boot may be made of leather, plastic, or nylon. It is fastened with buckles, laces, or straps. The wheels and a brake are attached to the bottom of the boot. The brake is usually a rubber pad behind the wheels at the heel of the skate. The

In-line skating is a fun and active sport.

skater can stop by lifting the toe of the skate so that the brake pad touches the ground.

In-line skating became popular in the mid-1980's. Many people enjoy in-line skating on city sidewalks and along pathways in parks. In-line skating is good exercise too. It keeps the skater's heart and lungs healthy. It also builds up the leg muscles. Some in-line skaters enter contests to show off their skills.

In-line skating is a fast sport. It is easy to pick up speed, and many in-line skaters have been hurt in falls. So it is important to always wear a helmet when in-line skating. It's also a good idea to wear pads on your knees and elbows, and wrist guards.

Other articles to read: **Roller skating; Skateboarding.**

Inoculation

Inoculations (*ih NAHK yuh LAY shuhns*) are shots or jabs. People sometimes get inoculations to protect them from a certain disease. The material in the shot helps people's bodies fight against the disease.

Many inoculations contain dead germs, or live germs that are too weak to cause disease. Others contain poisons that are treated so that they do not make a person sick.

Inoculations were first used in ancient China, India, and other places. In 1796, an English doctor called Edward Jenner began using inoculations. He protected people against a dangerous disease called smallpox.

Other articles to read: **Disease.**

Edward Jenner gave the first inoculation for smallpox to James Phipps in England in 1796.

Insect

● ●

Insects are small animals with six legs. Bees, ants, wasps, butterflies, cockroaches, and ladybugs are insects. So are mosquitoes, grasshoppers, and fleas.

There are about a million kinds of insects, and they live everywhere. Insects can be found in tropical jungles and in the Arctic cold. They live high in the mountains and in low, dry deserts.

Many people think that spiders are insects, but they aren't. Spiders have eight legs, but insects have six legs. A spider's body has two main parts, but an insect's body has three main parts. Also, most insects have wings and antennae (*an TEHN ee*), or long, thin feelers. Spiders have no antennae.

Some insects, like this moth, are beautifully colored.

The fairy fly is one of the tiniest insects. You need a magnifying glass to see it in real life.

The world of insects

Most insects are less than a quarter inch (6.4 millimeters) long. The smallest ones are fairy flies and some kinds of beetles. These insects are so tiny that they could fit through the eye of the smallest needle.

Some insects are much bigger. The Goliath beetle is more than 4 inches (10 centimeters) long. The Atlas moth can spread its wings about 10 inches (25 centimeters).

Insects come in every color of the rainbow. Some butterflies and moths have bright, colorful marks on their wings. Sometimes, the color of an insect helps it blend in with its surroundings. Beetles that live in the ground are black or brown. Some kinds of moths have the same color as tree bark.

Why insects are so successful

Almost every kind of animal must struggle to survive, or stay alive. Insects are good at surviving.

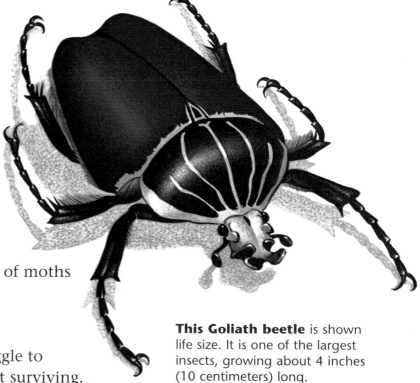

This Goliath beetle is shown life size. It is one of the largest insects, growing about 4 inches (10 centimeters) long.

Bees carry pollen from one plant to another.

Insects have been able to change so that they can live in the worst conditions. Some can live in very hot water. Some have been frozen solid—and still lived. Many insects can eat almost anything. Some will even eat cloth, cork, face powder, and paste.

Insects have also survived because they are small. They can hide from enemies in the tiniest places, and they don't need much to eat.

Most insects have wings, and they fly. This makes it easier for them to search for food and to get away from their enemies. Most insects lay many eggs, too. So they make many more of their own kind.

Why insects are important

Many insects help people. These insects are called beneficial (*behn uh FIHSH uhl*) insects. Bees, wasps, butterflies, and moths are beneficial insects. They pollinate plants, which means that they carry pollen from one plant to another. Plants use pollen to make seeds, which make more plants.

Make a Cricket Playground

Things You Need:
• aquarium or clear plastic box
• sponge
• scissors
• crackers or bread
• water
• small branches
• screen or loose cover
• paper
• 2 jar lids
• crickets

Crickets make fun pets. If your parents give you permission, you can get crickets from your yard or a pet store. And you can make a cricket playground for them.

Cut the sponge so that it fits into one of the lids. Moisten the sponge with water. The crickets will drink from the sponge. For snacks, crumble crackers or bread. Put the crumbs in the other lid.

Arrange branches here and there for your crickets to climb and jump on. Fold the paper to look like a tent.

Now, call your crickets out to play! Cover the "playground" with a loosely fitting cover or a screen, so that your crickets won't jump out.

Insects pollinate fruits, such as oranges, apples, and plums. They also pollinate vegetables such as peas, onions, carrots, and cabbages.

Insects are food for birds, fish, frogs, lizards, skunks, and many other animals. Some people eat insects. In South Africa, people roast termites and eat them like popcorn.

Some insects give us valuable products. Bees make honey and beeswax. Silk is made by silkworms.

Many insects help keep parks and gardens clean. They do this by eating animal wastes. They also eat dead animals and plants.

The adult firefly and the larva look very different.

The giant water bug grows to the size shown here.

Harmful insects

Of all the insects in the world, only a few are harmful to people. They do a lot of damage, though. Harmful insects damage plants and destroy crops. They can also cause damage in the home. Clothes moths and carpet beetles ruin clothing and rugs. Termites attack the wood in buildings. Some insects can spread disease when they bite. Certain kinds of mosquitoes spread malaria and other dangerous diseases.

The eastern subterranean termite lives underground.

The assassin bug has a nasty bite.

There are many ways to get rid of harmful insects. People swat flies and pick beetles off plants. Areas with lots of water are drained to keep mosquitoes away. Government workers try to keep harmful insects from coming into the country on airplanes and ships. Farmers use special farming methods that can prevent or stop insect damage. For example, they may plant or harvest crops when insects are few, or when the insects are not laying eggs.

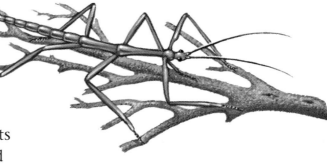

The walkingstick looks like a twig and so can easily hide from its enemies.

Sometimes, scientists bring predatory (*PREHD uh tuhr ee*) insects to problem areas. Predatory insects eat harmful insects. For example, ladybugs are predatory insects. They eat some of the insects that ruin crops. People often use chemicals to kill harmful insects, too.

The Carolina mantid can damage plants and destroy crops.

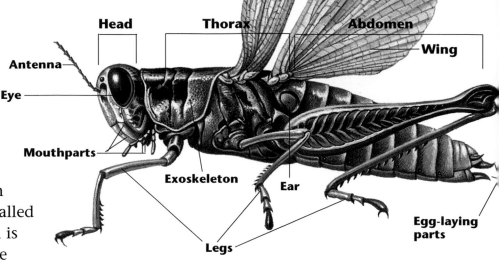

The visible parts of an insect
This is a female short-horned grasshopper.

The bodies of insects

An insect's body has three main parts. These parts are the head, the thorax (or middle section), and the abdomen. All insects also have a tough shell on the outside of their bodies. It is called the exoskeleton. The exoskeleton is like a suit of armor. It protects the insect's organs, or inside body parts.

The insect's head includes the mouthparts, eyes, and antennae. The mouthparts are used for feeding. Most adult insects have two huge eyes. But they cannot move or focus their eyes. They can only see things that are close to them. They have no eyelids, so their eyes are always open.

Almost all insects have two antennae between their eyes. They use their antennae to smell and to feel. They use smell to locate food and to find their way around. They also use smell to find a mate and a place to lay their eggs.

The thorax is the middle section of an insect's body. The insect's legs are attached to its thorax. All insects have three pairs of legs. The wings are attached to the thorax, too.

The insect's abdomen is used for digesting food. The parts used for mating are also in the abdomen. So are the parts for getting rid of waste and extra water.

Insects like these blister beetles use their antennae to smell and feel.

Most insects do not have ears. Instead, they have tiny hairs on their antennae or other parts of their body. These hairs shake when sound waves hit them. Crickets and long-horned grasshoppers have their "ears" on their front legs. Ants and male mosquitoes hear through their antennae.

Other articles to read: **Ant; Bee; Beetle; Butterfly; Caterpillar; Cicada; Cockroach; Cocoon; Cricket; Flea; Fly; Grasshopper; Locust; Louse; Moth; Termite; Wasp.**

Instinct

● ●

Instincts are natural feelings or knowledge that let living things perform certain actions. These actions do not have to be learned.

Instinctive actions are different from learned actions. Learned actions are a result of what happens to living things as they grow. Most actions are partly instinctive and partly learned. Many kinds of living things, including people, animals, fish, and insects, have instincts to behave in certain ways. Human babies do not have to learn how to suck a bottle. They have the instinct to suck.

When a living thing acts on its instinct, it usually needs something to make it act the way it does. This is called a stimulus (*STIHM yoo luhs*). When winter is near, the shorter days are the stimulus for a certain chemical to go through a bird's body. The chemical, in turn, is the stimulus in the bird's brain that tells it to fly to warmer places.

Instinct helps birds make their nests.

Most of the actions of insects, spiders, crabs, and lobsters are instinctive. These creatures are called lower animals. They act on instinct more than higher animals do. Higher animals include fish, amphibians, reptiles, birds, and mammals. Higher animals seem to use learning more than instinct as they grow.

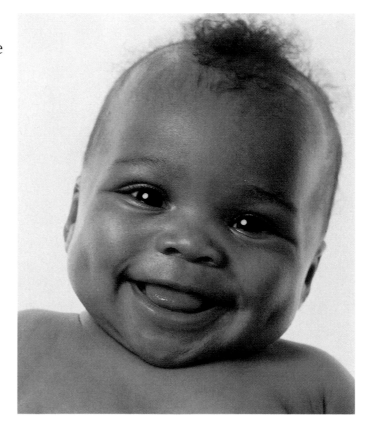

A baby's smile is part instinct, part learned behavior.

Insurance

● ●

Insurance helps protect people against large and unexpected costs. There are several kinds of insurance. Health insurance helps pay doctor and hospital bills when someone gets sick or hurt. Automobile insurance helps pay to fix or replace cars after an accident or a theft. Homeowner's or renter's insurance helps replace things that are stolen or damaged by such things as fire or water. Life insurance pays money to the family of the insured person if he or she dies.

People buy insurance from insurance companies. A person agrees to make regular payments to the insurance company. In return, the company pays if the person suffers a loss.

Insurance helps cover the cost when a house is damaged or destroyed by fire.

Intelligence

● ●

Intelligence is a word used to describe how quickly people are able to learn and understand things and how well and how long they remember ideas. Teachers may give students an IQ, or intelligence quotient, test to find out how intelligent they are. People have different levels of intelligence in different subjects. For example, someone who is good in mathematics may not be good at learning new words or understanding machinery.

Scientists disagree about where intelligence comes from. Every person is born with a certain amount of brain power. Many events in a child's life can affect that brain power. For example, infants who are poorly fed may not learn well. Also, children who are badly treated may become so upset that their intelligence fails to develop as it should.

IQ tests are used to measure intelligence.

Other articles to read: **Artificial intelligence.**

Internal combustion engine.

See **Engine**.

International trade

Internautional trade is the exchange of products between countries, or nations. It is different from domestic trade, which takes place entirely within a single country. International trade is sometimes called world trade or foreign trade.

With international trade, countries produce more of the things they are best able to make or grow. They buy other things they need from other countries. Important trade products include food, machines, and fuel. The things one nation sells to other nations are called exports. The things a nation buys are called imports. International trade makes it possible for people to buy a greater variety of products.

International trade is the exchange of goods and services between countries.

Internet

The Internet is a huge system of connected computers. It links businesses, colleges, organizations, and people throughout the world. The word *Internet* means *interconnected network of networks*.

The Internet connects thousands of smaller computer networks. These networks send out large amounts of information in the form of words, pictures, and sounds. Some schools use the Internet to get information for teachers and students.

To access, or get into, the Internet, you must have a computer with Internet software, or programming. You also need a piece of equipment called a modem (*MOH duhm*). The modem connects the computer to the network through telephone lines.

Much of the Internet works through worldwide networks of wires called fiber-optic cables (*FY buhr*

Fiber-optic cables carry data as flashes of light.

AHP tik KAY buhlz). These cables contain hair-thin threads of glass or plastic that carry data, or bits of information, as flashes of light. Fiber-optic cables can send much more data than regular phone lines made of copper wire.

Internet sources and uses

The Internet has information on just about every subject. You can search through many sources. Some information may be in a collection of data called a database (*DAY tuh bays*). Other information is shared on small electronic "bulletin boards," where people exchange messages with others who have similar interests.

People also can send personal messages through the Internet, as if they were talking to one another. Messages may be a few short words or a long letter or report. These messages are called electronic mail or e-mail. People use an Internet "address" to send and receive e-mail.

Other uses of the Internet include getting the latest news and playing games. One part of the Internet, known as the World Wide Web, provides pictures and sometimes even sound to make the information in its documents, or reports, more interesting and useful.

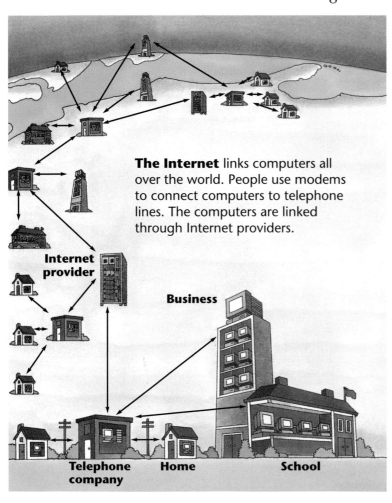

The Internet links computers all over the world. People use modems to connect computers to telephone lines. The computers are linked through Internet providers.

Internet provider

Business

Telephone company   Home   School

Beginnings of the Internet

The Internet began in the 1960's. The United States Department of Defense developed a network of military and government computers. This network was intended to protect the information in those computers in case of a war, or a disaster such as an earthquake or flood. Soon the governments of other countries began to join the United States network.

Universities and other organizations also developed their own computer networks. Later, these networks were joined with the government network to form the Internet. Today, the Internet is open to everyone.

The future of the Internet

The Internet will continue to develop as computer technology becomes more powerful. It may become part of an even bigger network called the information superhighway, which would connect computers with telephone companies, cable-TV stations, and other communication systems. Then people could bank, shop, watch TV, and do many other things through the network.

Inuit

The Inuit (*IHN yoo iht*) are a group of people who live in the Arctic—the far northern part of the world. Their homeland stretches from the northeastern tip of Russia across Alaska and northern Canada to Greenland. The Inuit live farther north than any other people on Earth.

The Inuit used to be called Eskimos. Many Inuit do not like the word *Eskimo*. It comes from a Native American word that means "someone who

The Inuit catch fish by spearing them through holes in the ice.

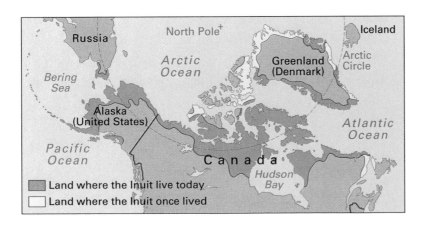

Land where the Inuit live today
Land where the Inuit once lived

Inuit homeland

On winter hunting trips, the Inuit survive their harsh Arctic world by building houses of snow and burning animal blubber for fuel.

eats raw meat" or "someone who speaks a foreign language." The name *Inuit* comes from the Inuit-Inupiaq language and means "the people" or "real people." The Inuit word for just one person is *Inuk*.

The Inuit live in one of the coldest parts of the world. Average temperatures in the Arctic region are below freezing for nine to ten months each year. The land is covered with snow most of the time. The rivers and lakes—and even the sea itself—stay frozen for much of the year.

Most kinds of plants and animals cannot live as far north as the Inuit do. Seals, walruses, whales, and polar bears live in the sea, on the sea ice, and along the shores of the Arctic Ocean. Some birds and other animals live on land in the Arctic during the summer but then go south for the winter. Animals of the Arctic include wolves, foxes, hares, musk oxen, and a kind of large deer called the caribou (*KAR ih boo*). Arctic fish include arctic char, arctic cod, lake trout, salmon, and whitefish.

The Inuit today

More than 100,000 Inuit live in Russia, Alaska, Canada, and Greenland. Most Inuit speak English, Russian, or Danish as well as their own language. Many Inuit are Christians.

Most Inuit live in towns or in small groups scattered along the coast of the Arctic Ocean. They have wooden homes and wear modern clothing. They travel by motorboat in the water and by snowmobile on land. Many Inuit hunt and fish to feed their families.

Some Inuit have jobs in the fishing industry. Others make soapstone carvings and other artwork and crafts. Some work in mines. But many Inuit cannot find jobs, so the government of the country they live in provides health care, homes, and schools for them.

The old way of life

The old, or traditional, Inuit way of life began

about 1,000 years ago. At that time, the Inuit lived in what is now the Bering Sea region of Alaska and Siberia. The old way of life lasted until the early 1900's.

The Inuit caught fish and hunted seals, walruses, and whales in the ocean. On land, they hunted caribou, musk oxen, polar bears, and many smaller animals. They ate the meat of these animals and used the skins to make clothes and tents. They made tools and weapons from the animals' bones, horns, and teeth.

Most Inuit families had both a summer house and a winter house. The summer house was a tent framed with wood and covered with seal or caribou skins. The winter house had walls made of rocks and sod, or pieces of dirt covered with grass. The roof was made from wooden boards or whalebone and covered with sod. When they hunted animals during the winter, Inuit hunters built dome-shaped snowhouses to live in for a short time as they followed the animals.

During winter months, most Inuit traveled on sleds pulled by dogs. In summer, people walked over land and traveled in long, narrow boats called kayaks (*KY aks*) or larger boats called umiaks (*OO mee aks*).

Other articles to read: **Alaska; Arctic; Arctic Ocean; Canada; Greenland; Russia.**

Inuit clothing

Outer clothing   Inner clothing

Hooded Jacket

Mitten

Trousers

Boots

Inuit transportation

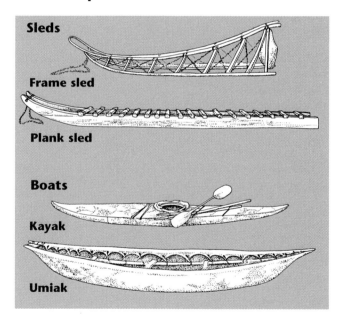

Sleds

Frame sled

Plank sled

Boats

Kayak

Umiak

Inuit houses

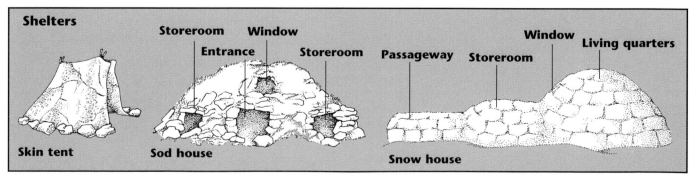

Shelters

Storeroom   Window

Entrance   Storeroom   Passageway   Storeroom

Window   Living quarters

Skin tent   Sod house   Snow house

Invention

● ◄

Important inventions in history	
Plow	5000-3000 B.C.
Wheel	3500 B.C.
Magnetic compass	300's B.C.
Paper	By A.D. 1
Movable type	About 1440
Telescope	1608
Steam engine	1690-1769
Steamboat	1787-1807
Cotton gin	1793
Steam locomotive	1804
Photography	1826
Gas refrigeration	1834
Telegraph	1837
Sewing machine	1846
Dynamite	1867
Typewriter	1867
Electric motor	1873
Telephone	1876
Phonograph	1877
Incandescent light	1879
Gasoline automobile	1885
Zipper	1893
Motion picture	mid-1890's
Radio	1895
Airplane	1903
Television	1920's
Radar	About 1935
Atomic bomb	1945
Digital computer	1946
Laser	1960
Microprocessor	1971
CD player	1983

An invention is the creation of something new, such as a tool or a machine, or a new way of getting work done. Inventions may give people greater control over their environment and allow them to live better, easier, and happier lives.

An invention is different from a discovery. A discovery is seeing something that exists in nature for the first time. An invention is the creation of something that never existed before. For example, people discovered fire, but they invented the match to start a fire.

**Wheel
3500 B.C.**

People may invent things to make money, but the main reason for invention is to help people. An invention must fill an economic, military, or social need. Economic needs have led to the invention of many tools and machines used on farms and in factories and businesses. Military needs have led to the invention of weapons used in war. Social needs have led to the invention of tools used by doctors and products used in people's homes. If an invention does not fill one of these needs, people will not use it.

People have invented things since the earliest times. For example, the plow and the wheel were invented more than 5,000 years ago, and paper was invented about 2,000 years ago. But many important inventions have been developed in the

**Airplane
1903**

last 600 years. For example, modern printing was invented in about the year 1440.

Thousands of inventions were created in the 1800's to make life at home easier and more comfortable. These inventions included the gas refrigerator (1834), the sewing machine (1846), the safety pin (1849), the telephone (1876), the phonograph (1877), the electric light bulb (1879), the gasoline-powered car (1885), the zipper (1893), and the radio (1895). Important inventions of the 1900's included the airplane (1903), television (1920's), modern plastics (mid-1930's), and the microprocessor used to control modern computers (1971).

**CD Player
1984**

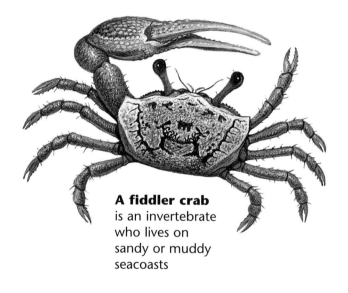

A fiddler crab is an invertebrate who lives on sandy or muddy seacoasts

The fluke, a tiny parasite, is an invertebrate

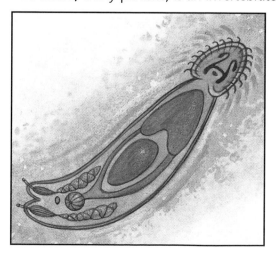

Invertebrate

Invertebrates (*ihn VUR tuh brihts*) are animals without backbones. The bones that make up the backbone are called vertebrae (*VUR tuh bray*). Invertebrate means *without a backbone.* Animals with backbones are called vertebrates.

There are many kinds of invertebrates. The biggest group includes insects, spiders, and crayfish. Other animals with jointed legs and hard outer skeletons belong to this group too.

The purple sea urchin is an invertebrate found in the Pacific Coast of North America.

Another group includes jellyfish, sea anemones, and coral. Sponges, sea animals with many pores (*pohrz*), or holes, are another kind. Still other groups include flat-bodied worms, round-bodied worms, worms with sections such as earthworms, and sea animals such as starfish.

Other articles to read: **Arthropod; Insect; Mollusk; Sponge; Vertebrate; Worm.**

Iowa

● ●

Des Moines

★

Iowa (blue) ranks 25th in size among the states.

IOWA

State flag

State seal

Iowa is a state in the Midwestern region of the United States. Wisconsin and Illinois lie to the east. South Dakota and Nebraska are to the west. Minnesota forms Iowa's northern border. Missouri lies to the south. Iowa produces so much corn that it is called the *Corn State.*

Des Moines is the capital and largest city in Iowa. It lies in the south-central part of the state where the Des Moines and Raccoon rivers meet. Des Moines is an important manufacturing center. Cedar Rapids, Iowa's second largest city, is also a big manufacturing center. Dubuque is a port city on the west bank of the Mississippi River.

Iowa farms produce hogs, corn, beef cattle, and soybeans.

Land. A million years ago, glaciers (*GLAY shuhrz*) covered Iowa. These great sheets of ice moved very slowly over the land. They flattened the land and filled the valleys. The glaciers also made the soil very rich. Today, most of Iowa is a flat plain.

Only one glacier moved across the northeast part of Iowa. Here, the land has pine-covered cliffs and hills.

The Mississippi River flows along the eastern border of Iowa. Near the Mississippi are deep valleys and limestone cliffs. Hardwood trees grow in the river valleys. Small lakes and streams are scattered across northern and northwestern Iowa. People who love the outdoors enjoy hiking in these areas.

Resources and products. Farms cover almost all of Iowa's land. Corn and soybeans are the most important crops. Much of the corn crop feeds the livestock. Other crops include oats, hay, flaxseed, rye, and wheat.

Iowa farmers also grow many different vegetables, especially cabbages, cucumbers, green beans, onions, potatoes, and tomatoes. Apples are the biggest fruit crop. Iowa farmers also raise livestock, such as hogs and cattle.

Most of Iowa's manufacturing plants make food products from the crops and livestock grown in the state. These include canned ham, breakfast sausage, corn oil, cornstarch, corn sugar, and dairy products. Iowa factories also make farm machinery, such as tractors, and household appliances, such as refrigerators.

Important dates in Iowa

Indian days	Native Americans lived in the Iowa region long before Europeans arrived. Ancient Indians known as mound builders buried their dead in large mounds. Many of these mounds can be seen today.
1673	Explorers Louis Jolliet and Jacques Marquette of France traveled into the Iowa region.
1788	Julien Dubuque, Iowa's first white settler, began mining lead near present-day Dubuque.
1803	The United States purchased the Louisiana Territory from France. This huge region, which included present-day Iowa, spread from the Mississippi River to the Rocky Mountains.
1832	Indians led by Chief Black Hawk were defeated by the U.S. Army in the Black Hawk War.
1833	Permanent settlements began in the Iowa region.
1838	Congress created the Territory of Iowa.
1846	Iowa became the 29th state on December 28.
1867	The first railroad was completed across Iowa, from the Mississippi River to Council Bluffs.
1917	Iowa began a large road-building program.
1960	The U.S. government reported that, for the first time, more Iowans lived in cities than on farms.
1993	Heavy rains caused the Mississippi and other rivers to flood in Iowa. These floods caused great damage to buildings and farms.

The first railroad to cross Iowa was completed in 1867.

Other articles to read: **Black Hawk; Jolliet, Louis; Louisiana Purchase; Marquette, Jacques; Mississippi River; Mound builders.**

Facts About Iowa

Capital: Des Moines.

Area: 56,276 sq. mi. (145,754 km²).

Population: 2,787,424.

Year of statehood: 1846.

State abbreviations: Ia. (traditional), IA (postal).

State motto: *Our Liberties We Prize and Our Rights We Will Maintain.*

State song: "The Song of Iowa." Words by S. H. M. Byers; sung to the tune of "Der Tannenbaum."

Largest cities: Des Moines, Cedar Rapids, Davenport.

Government:
State government:
Governor: 4-year term.
State senators: 50;
  4-year terms.
State representatives: 100;
  2-year terms.
Counties: 99.
Federal government:
U.S. senators: 2.
U.S. representatives: 5.
Electoral votes: 7.

State bird
Eastern goldfinch
(American goldfinch)

State flower
Wild rose

Iran

● ○

Facts About Iran

Capital: Teheran.

Area: 630,557 sq. mi. (1,633,188 km²).

Population: Estimated 1998 population— 71,569,000.

Official language: Persian, also called Farsi.

Climate:
Hot summers, cooler on Caspian Sea coast and in mountains. Cool winters, cold on plateau and in mountains. Caspian Sea coast is rainy in summer.

Chief products:
Agriculture: barley, nuts, rice, sugar beets, wheat.
Manufacturing: bricks, cement, cloth, food products, petroleum products.

Form of government: Republic.

Flag

Iran (*ih RAHN*) is a country in southwestern Asia, in the area of the world known as the Middle East. South of Iran lie the Persian Gulf and the Gulf of Oman, which flow into the Indian Ocean. Iraq and Turkey border Iran to the west. Armenia, Azerbaijan, the Caspian Sea, and Turkmenistan lie to the north. Afghanistan and Pakistan are to the east. Iran is one of the world's oldest countries. Teheran is the country's capital and largest city.

Land. About half of Iran is made up of a high, flat piece of land called a plateau (*plah TOH*). Two huge deserts stretch across the plateau. They are among the world's driest deserts. Few plants and animals, and almost no people, live there.

Two mountain ranges, the Elburz and the Zagros, surround most of the plateau. In the north, a narrow strip of coastland lies between the Elburz Mountains and the Caspian Sea. In the west, a plain lies between the Zagros Mountains and the border of Iraq.

People. More than half of the people in Iran are Persians. Most Iranians speak the Persian language, also called Farsi. It is used in schools and by the Iranian government.

Most Iranians live in the northwestern part of the country, along the Caspian Sea, and in and near Teheran. Some city people live in apartment buildings, and others live in traditional houses. Most families in the countryside live in traditional houses. These houses are made of dried mud or brick and have a flat roof covered with mud or straw. The main foods of Iran's people are rice and bread. Sometimes the rice is mixed with meat and vegetables.

Nearly all the people of Iran are Muslims, people who follow the faith of Islam. The government makes strict laws according to Islam. These laws control much of what people may say or do. The government says that women should wear a long black veil, called a chador. It covers the entire body. It also covers the head and is sometimes drawn across the lower face.

Resources and products. About half of all Iran's workers have service jobs. Service jobs include jobs in the government, in hospitals, in schools, in banks, and in restaurants. About one-fourth of Iran's workers hold jobs in factories. The country's main factory products are bricks, cement, cloth, food products, and petroleum products.

Iran is one of the world's leading producers of petroleum. People around the world use petroleum for running cars and for other purposes. Nearly all Iran's income comes from petroleum.

Iran and its neighbors

About one-fourth of the workers in Iran are farmers. Most of them live along the Caspian Sea coast or on the plain near Iraq. Farmers raise such crops as barley, corn, cotton, dates and other fruits, lentils, nuts, rice, sugar beets, tea, tobacco, and wheat. Cattle, goats, and sheep provide milk and meat. Iranian fishing crews catch a variety of fish in the Caspian Sea and the Persian Gulf.

History. People have lived in what is now Iran for more than 5,000 years. The greatest early kingdom in Iran was the Persian Empire. It was founded about 2,500 years ago and lasted about 200 years. Persian

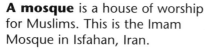
A mosque is a house of worship for Muslims. This is the Imam Mosque in Isfahan, Iran.

The Elburz Mountains

kings once ruled most of southwestern Asia as well as parts of Europe and Africa.

Other countries have taken over Iran many times during its long history. One of the most important invasions happened in the middle of the 600's, when Muslim Arabs conquered Iran. Under their rule, most of the people became Muslims. From the 1500's to 1700's, the Safavid rulers of Iran controlled a powerful empire.

Crude oil was discovered in southwestern Iran in the early 1900's. When Iran began to sell petroleum to other countries, the nation became rich. In 1979, a group of people led by Ayatollah Ruhollah Khomeini, a Muslim religious leader, took control of the government away from the *shah,* or king, Mohammad Reza Pahlavi. Ayatollah Khomeini set up a new government based on Islamic law, with himself as the most powerful leader.

In 1980, a war broke out between Iran and Iraq. In 1988, the two countries agreed to stop fighting.

Ayatollah Khomeini died in 1989, and another Muslim leader, Ayatollah Ali Khamanei, became an important figure in Iran's government. Iran now has a president who heads the government.

Other articles to read: **Caspian Sea; Islam; Muslims; Persia, Ancient; Teheran.**

Iraq

• •

Iraq is a country of southwestern Asia, in the area of the world known as the Middle East. The southeastern tip of Iraq lies on the Persian Gulf. Iraq's neighbors are Iran to the east, Kuwait and Saudi Arabia to the south, Jordan and Syria to the west, and Turkey to the north. Baghdad is Iraq's capital and largest city.

Land. Mountains rise along northeastern Iraq. South of the mountains, a vast plain stretches southeast across the country to the Persian Gulf. Some parts of the plain are dry and hilly, some parts are flat land with farms and oil fields, and other parts are swampland. The Tigris and Euphrates rivers flow through the plain. People use water from the rivers to grow crops. A sandy, hilly desert covers the southwestern and western parts of the country. Iraq gets very little rain.

People. Most of the people in Iraq are Arabs, a Middle Eastern people who speak Arabic. The Kurds, who have their own Kurdish language, make up a smaller group. Most Kurds also speak Arabic, which is Iraq's official language. Nearly all the people of Iraq are Muslims, people who follow the faith of Islam.

Facts About Iraq

Capital: Baghdad.

Area: 169,235 sq. mi. (438,317 km²).

Population: Estimated 1998 population—22,345,000.

Official language: Arabic.

Climate: Hot summers, cool winters, and little rain. Hottest temperatures and driest weather in the deserts of the east and southeast.

Chief products:

Agriculture: barley, dates, grapes, rice, tomatoes, wheat.

Manufacturing: building materials, chemicals, cloth, flour, iron and steel, leather goods, petroleum refining.

Mining: petroleum.

Form of government: Republic.

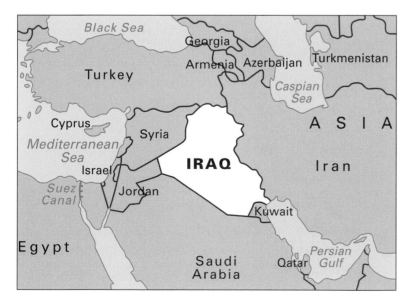

Iraq and its neighbors

Flag

Most of Iraq's people live in cities on the plain. Many city people live in apartment buildings.

Most people in the countryside live in small houses. In the north, the houses are made of stone. In the south, the houses are made of dried mud and brick. A few people in western Iraq are nomads, or wanderers, who move from place to place with their camels, goats, and sheep.

In the cities, wealthy people dress in modern clothing like the clothing worn in the United States and much of Europe. Other people wear the kind of clothing that has been worn in Iraq for hundreds of years. Men wear long cotton robes and jackets, and women wear a long robe with a scarf that covers much of the head.

The main foods in Iraq are rice and bread. The people also eat many kinds of fruits, vegetables, meat, and fish. A common food in Iraq is sanbusak, a moon-shaped dough stuffed with cheese or meat. Popular drinks include tea, coffee, and fruit juices.

Resources and products. About half the workers in Iraq have service jobs. Wealthy people often have service jobs in business and government. Other service workers have jobs in banks and offices.

Many of Iraq's workers have jobs in the oil industry or in factories. Iraq's factories make cement, chemicals, cloth, iron, processed foods, soap, and steel.

Much of the land in Iraq is too dry for farming, so few people in Iraq work as farmers. Farm crops include barley, dates, grapes, rice, tomatoes, and wheat.

History. The world's first known civilization, or organized social group of people living in cities, developed about 5,500 years

Dry grazing lands cover much of Iraq's northern plain.

Baghdad is the capital of Iraq.

ago in Sumer, along the Tigris and Euphrates rivers. Sumer was part of Mesopotamia, an area that included most of what is now Iraq and parts of Syria and Turkey.

In the year 637, Arab Muslims took over Mesopotamia. In the 700's, the Arabs founded Baghdad as their capital of their empire. By 800, Baghdad had grown into a city of more than a million people and was a world center of trade and culture.

In 1258, Mongol warriors from central Asia came to Mesopotamia and destroyed the Arab Empire. From the 1500's through the 1800's, the Ottoman Empire ruled Mesopotamia. The Ottoman Empire was ruled from what is now Turkey.

British troops took Mesopotamia from the Ottomans during World War I (1914-1918). In 1932, Iraq became independent, or free from British control.

In 1980, a war broke out between Iraq and Iran. In 1988, the two countries agreed to stop fighting.

In 1990, troops from Iraq took over Kuwait, a small country south of Iraq. The United Nations (UN) told Iraq to withdraw the troops, but Iraq would not withdraw, and the Persian Gulf War broke out in March 1991. UN forces, led by the United States, defeated Iraq's army. The war ended in April 1991.

Other articles to read: **Persian Gulf War.**

Ireland

● ●

Ireland is a small country in northwestern Europe. It lies on an island in the North Atlantic Ocean. The island is also called Ireland. Dublin is the country's capital and largest city.

Land. Ireland is known as the Emerald Isle because of its beautiful green countryside. Farmlands cover much of the central part of the country, and mountains rise near the coasts.

People. Most of the Irish people are white Europeans, and nearly all of them are Roman Catholic Christians. All the people speak English. Some also speak the ancient Irish language. More than half of Ireland's people live in cities and large towns. Some live in brick or concrete houses, and others live in apartment buildings.

Potatoes have been an important food in Ireland for several hundred years. One of Ireland's most famous dishes is Irish stew, made with potatoes, onions, and beef or mutton, the meat of sheep.

Resources and products. More than half of Ireland's workers have jobs that provide services to people. They work in schools, hospitals, restaurants, hotels, and other businesses. Factories in Ireland make beer, chemicals, clothing, computers, machines, medicines, paper, and processed foods.

Most of Ireland's farmland is used as pasture for cattle, sheep, and horses. Farmers also grow barley, hay, potatoes, sugar beets, and wheat. The waters along Ireland's coasts are excellent fishing areas.

History. The first people to live in Ireland probably came to the island from the European mainland about 8,000 years ago. About 2,400 years ago, people called Celts came to Ireland from England and the European mainland. The Celts spoke the Irish language, and they created beautiful artwork by carving patterns in stone. Saint Patrick brought

Facts About Ireland

Capital: Dublin.

Area: 27,137 sq. mi. (70,284 km²).

Population: Estimated 1998 population— 3,590,000.

Official languages: English and Irish.

Climate: Mild and wet.

Chief products:

Agriculture: barley, beef and dairy cattle, hogs, horses, potatoes, poultry, sheep, sugar beets, wheat.

Manufacturing: alcoholic beverages, chemicals, cloth and clothing, computers, machinery, medicines, metal products, paper, printed materials, processed foods.

Form of government: Republic.

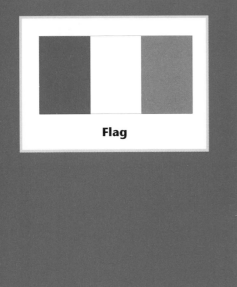

Flag

Christianity to Ireland about 1,600 years ago.

Over the years, many other groups took control of all or part of Ireland. These groups included the Vikings, the Normans, and the English.

From 1845 to 1848, a plant disease killed Ireland's potatoes, the people's main food. About 1 million Irish people died of starvation or disease. More than 1 million others left Ireland. Many of these people moved to the United States and Canada to look for food and jobs.

In 1919, fighting broke out between Ireland's British rulers and Irish people who wanted the country to be free. In 1920, the British government divided Ireland into two parts. An area in the northeast corner of the island became known as Northern Ireland. Like the British, most of the people in Northern Ireland were Protestant Christians. In 1921, the rest of Ireland became the Irish Free State. Most of the people in the Irish Free State were Roman Catholic Christians.

In 1949, Ireland cut any remaining ties to Britain. It was named the Republic of Ireland. Today, many people in Ireland want Northern Ireland to join with Ireland again. But most of Northern Ireland's people want to stay separate.

Other articles to read: **Blarney Stone; Celts; Dublin; Northern Ireland; Saint Patrick's Day.**

Ireland is called the Emerald Isle because of its lush, green landscape.

Ireland and its neighbors

North Atlantic Ocean

North Sea

Denmark

IRELAND

United Kingdom

Netherlands

Belgium

Germany

Luxembourg

EUROPE

Switzerland

France

Iron and steel

Steelmakers change pellets of concentrated ore into pig iron. Then, they change the pig iron into steel.

Iron and steel are the cheapest and most useful metals in the world. They are used in thousands of products, from paper clips to cars.

Iron is one of the most common kinds of material in the earth. It is found in minerals or rocks called ores (*ohrz*). People dig huge holes in the ground called mines to get the ores.

To make iron we can use, the ore is heated until it melts. The iron then separates from other materials in the ore.

Many products are made from iron. Steel is made from iron, too. To make steel, the iron is heated again and some materials are added. This produces liquid steel. The liquid steel is then formed into sheets, rods, and other shapes. These shapes are used to make many products.

Other articles to read: **Welding**.

Irrigation

Irrigation is used to grow crops in the Negev Desert, one of Israel's driest regions.

Irrigation is the watering of land with water other than rain. People bring water from lakes, rivers, streams, and wells to irrigate land that does not get enough rain.

In desert regions, such as Egypt and the Southwestern United States, farming would be impossible without irrigation. In areas where it is rainy part of the year but dry part of the year, such as Italy and California, irrigation allows farming to continue during the dry season. Even places with regular rainfall, such as Western Europe and the Eastern United States, sometimes have a drought (*drowt*), or a long period without rain. Then irrigation is needed to save the crops.

To use irrigation, people must find ways to bring water from its source to where it is needed.

Most farms use a network of canals to carry water from streams, rivers, and lakes to ditches that take the water to the fields. Water from wells is often pumped to the surface. The pump in the well lifts the water into a ditch or pipe that carries it to the crops.

Irrigation water may be flooded over the surface of the field or sprayed over the field with sprinklers. It may be dripped onto the field through plastic tubes on the ground or soaked into the plant roots from underground pipes. The water used for irrigation must be fresh, not salty, water.

Flood irrigation covers a field with water. Workers tend to rice plants in a flooded field in India.

Islam

Islam is one of the world's major religions. People who follow the faith of Islam are called Muslims. More than half the world's Muslims live in South and Southeast Asia. Indonesia, India, Bangladesh, and Pakistan have the largest Muslim populations. About one-fourth of all Muslims live in the Middle East. There are many Muslims in parts of Europe and several million in the United States.

Islam was first preached by an Arab prophet, or holy man, named Muhammad. In about 610, he began to receive messages from *Allah,* or God. Muhammad preached that there is only one God and that God wants people to make *Islam,* or submission, to God.

Muhammad died in 632, but the new religion of Islam soon spread. By the mid-700's, Muslims had built an empire that stretched from the Atlantic Ocean to the borders of China. Muhammad's teachings are written down in the *Quran* (also spelled *Koran),* the holy book of Islam. The sign of Islam is a crescent, or a thin moon, and a star.

Muslims follow the Five Pillars of Islam: (1) saying they believe in Allah, the one God, and Muhammad as a prophet; (2) praying five times

The symbol of Islam is a crescent and a star.

a day; (3) giving alms, such as money or gifts, to the poor; (4) fasting, or not eating or drinking, from sunrise to sunset every day during Ramadan, a holy month of the Islamic year; and (5) making a pilgrimage, or holy journey, to Mecca, the birthplace of Muhammad in Saudi Arabia, at least once during their life. The building where Muslims worship together is called a mosque (*mahsk*).

Other articles to read: **Mecca; Muhammad; Muslims; Ramadan.**

Muslim pilgrims worship at a mosque at Mecca, the birthplace of Muhammad in Saudi Arabia.

Continental islands are pieces of land that once were connected to a continent.

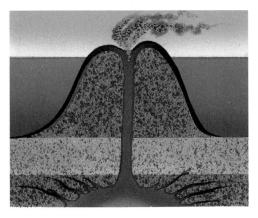

Volcanic islands are formed by volcanoes on the ocean floor.

Island

An island (*EYE land*) is a piece of land that is surrounded by water. It is smaller than a continent. Islands are found in oceans, rivers, and lakes throughout the world.

Islands may be small or large. Some islands cover a smaller area than a city block. A small island is called an islet (*EYE liht*). The largest island in the world is Greenland, in the North Atlantic Ocean. Greenland is slightly larger than Mexico.

The difference between an island and a continent is based on size. Like an island, Australia is surrounded by water. But Australia is more than three times bigger than Greenland, the largest island. Because of its size, Australia is called a continent rather than an island.

Islands make up the entire land area of some countries, including Japan and the Philippines.

Millions of people live on such islands. Other islands have no people at all. Some of these islands are refuges, or safe places, for birds and wild animals.

Throughout history, islands have served as stopping places for travelers and traders in ships. So islands have helped the spread of people, animals, and plants from one continent to another.

Some islands were formed hundreds of millions of years ago. But new ones are forming all the time. There are five main kinds of islands: (1) continental islands, (2) tectonically formed islands, (3) volcanic islands, (4) coral islands, and (5) barrier islands. Each kind is formed in a different way.

Coral islands are created by coral reefs. A reef may grow around a sinking volcano.

Some continental islands are pieces of land that were once part of a continent. Some of these islands became separated from the continent when water covered the land between the continent and the island. Others became separated when their connection with the continent was worn away. Tectonically formed islands are created by movements of Earth's crust. Earth's crust, or outer rocky part, consists of huge plates that move very slowly. When one plate is pushed under another plate, the top plate may scrape off pieces of the bottom plate. Over millions of years, this material piles up to form an island. Volcanic islands are formed by volcanoes under the sea. Coral islands are created by coral reefs—limestone formations made by tiny creatures—that grow in a ring around a sinking volcanic island. Barrier islands are formed when winds and ocean waves pile up sand, dirt, and rocks into long, narrow islands along a seacoast.

Barrier islands are created from sand and soil that build up along a shoreline.

Israel

● ●

Israel is a small country in southwestern Asia. It lies on a thin strip of land on the shore of the Mediterranean Sea. It is bordered by Egypt, Jordan, Syria, and Lebanon. Jerusalem is Israel's capital and largest city.

Land. Israel has four major land regions. The coastal plain is a thin strip of land along the Mediterranean Sea. Most of Israel's people live in this area. Most of the nation's factories and farms are here too.

The Judeo-Galilean Highlands include a series of mountain ranges in northern and central Israel. The highlands include the area known as the West Bank. Galilee is home to most of Israel's Arabs. Jerusalem is located in the northern part of the Judean Hills.

The Rift Valley is a long, thin strip of land in eastern Israel. The area includes the Dead Sea, a saltwater lake. The shore of the Dead Sea is the lowest land area on Earth. The Jordan River flows through the Rift Valley.

The Negev Desert is a dry area of flatlands and mountains in southern Israel. Water from the Sea of Galilee is now being pumped to parts of the Negev. This allows farmers to grow some crops here.

Facts About Israel

Capital: Jerusalem.

Area: 8,130 sq. mi. (21,056 km^2), not including 2,700 sq. mi. (7,000 km^2) of Arab land occupied since 1967.

Population: Estimated 1998 population—5,883,000.

Official languages: Hebrew and Arabic.

Climate: Hot, dry summers; mild winters. Temperatures are cooler at high land. Rain falls mainly from November to March.

Chief products:

Agriculture: citrus and other fruits, cotton, eggs, grains, poultry, vegetables.

Manufacturing: chemical products, cloth and clothing, electronic equipment, fertilizer, finished diamonds, paper, plastics, processed foods, scientific and optical instruments.

Mining: potash, bromine, salt, phosphates.

Form of government: Democratic republic.

Israel and its neighbors

People. Most of Israel's people are Jews. Some of Israel's Jewish people were born in Israel. Others have come from countries all around the world.

Most of the other people who live in Israel are Arabs. Generally, Israel's Jewish and Arab groups do not trust one another. They live in separate areas, go to separate schools, speak different languages, and follow different traditions.

Resources and products. Israel has few natural resources, but the people of Israel live well. Many people have come to Israel from other countries. They have started businesses that have helped the country. Also, other countries have given money to help Israel grow.

Most of Israel's people make their money in businesses that provide services. These businesses include banks, restaurants, and hotels.

Israel has many modern factories. The goods they produce include computers, paper products, and food products.

History. Both the Jews and the Arabs trace their history back to Abraham, who settled in what is now Israel nearly 4,000 years ago. Over the centuries, many people have conquered and controlled Israel. About 3,000 years ago, the Kingdom of Israel reached its greatest strength under King David and his son King Solomon. After Solomon

Flag

The Dome of the Rock is in Jerusalem. This shrine marks the place from which Muhammad rose to the throne of God. This Muslim shrine is built on the site of the Jewish Temple.

This moshav, a group of farms, is in the Galilee region of Israel. Each family farms its own land, but the village provides supplies and sells the crops.

died, the kingdom divided into two parts—Israel in the north and Judah in the south. The word *Jew* came from the name Judah. During the next 1,000 years, the Jews were conquered by several empires.

In 63 B.C., the Roman Empire invaded Judah. The Romans eventually forced most Jews to leave the region. The Romans named the region Palestina, which became Palestine in English.

In the 600's, Muslim Arabs took over the area. From that time until the mid-1900's, most of the people in Palestine were Arabs.

In the late 1800's, many European Jews wanted to start a Jewish state in Palestine. Jews began arriving in Palestine in large numbers. By the early 1900's, fights started between the Jews and Arabs. In 1947, the United Nations (UN) decided to divide the area into an Arab state and a Jewish state. Israel was founded in 1948 as a homeland for Jews from all parts of the world. Ever since, there have been problems between Israel and the Arab nations around Israel. While the two sides have worked for peace over the years, disagreements continue.

Other articles to read: **Gaza Strip; Jerusalem; Jews; Meir, Golda; West Bank.**

Italy

Italy is a country in southern Europe. It is bordered by Austria, France, Slovenia, and Switzerland. It is made up of a boot-shaped peninsula that extends into the Mediterranean Sea. A peninsula is a strip of land with water on three sides. Rome is the capital and largest city of Italy.

Land. Italy has two groups of mountains, the Alps and the Apennines. The Alps form Italy's northern border. The Apennines stretch almost all the way from the north to the south of Italy. Italy also has many valleys and plains. Most of Italy's people live in the Po River Valley in northern Italy. Sicily, the largest island in the Mediterranean Sea, lies off the southwest coast. Mount Etna, one of the largest active volcanoes in the world, is in Sicily.

Italy and its neighbors

Facts About Italy

Capital: Rome.

Area: 116,320 sq. mi. (301,268 km²).

Population: Estimated 1998 population— 57,221,000.

Official language: Italian.

Climate: Central and southern Italy have hot summers and mild winters. The summers are dry. Northern Italy is also hot in the summer but much cooler in winter. The north receives rain all year around. The mountains are cold and snowy in winter.

Chief products:

Agriculture: beef cattle, corn, grapes, hogs, olives, oranges, tomatoes, wheat.

Manufacturing: chemicals, clothing and shoes, foods and beverages, machinery, motor vehicles, petroleum products.

Mining: granite, marble, natural gas.

Form of government: Parliamentary democracy.

Flag

People. Most Italian people live in apartment buildings. Some people live in single-family homes. Most people live with their parents until they get married. Grandparents often help care for children.

Italian people enjoy large meals with several courses or dishes. The first dish is often pasta or soup. The main course may be meat or fish. Pizza is a popular snack or light meal. Fruit is a popular dessert, and wine is often served with the meal.

Many Italians watch and play soccer. On weekends, the parks are filled with soccer teams. Basketball is also popular.

Resources and products. Since 1945, Italy has made most of its money from modern businesses such as automobile factories, banks, and airlines. Millions of tourists come to Italy, so restaurants and hotels are also important. In the

The Alps form Italy's northern border. Italian winter ski resorts are popular.

past, farming was very important, and the grapes grown in the Po Valley are still important for making wine. Italy has earned more money since it joined the European Community, a group of European countries that trade and cooperate with one another.

History. About 2,500 years ago, the city of Rome started to grow in importance. The Romans built a great empire that ruled many countries. About 1,500 years ago, groups from northern Europe began fighting the Romans. The last Roman emperor lost his power in the year 476.

The Italian city of Florence is famous for its art and architecture.

For hundreds of years, various groups fought for control of Italy. Emperors from Germany ruled it part of the time. The popes, who headed the Roman Catholic Church, also ruled part of Italy.

After the year 1000, some Italian cities like Venice, Milan, and Florence became powerful and wealthy states. These city-states often fought wars with each other. During the time called the Renaissance—in the 1300's, 1400's, and 1500's—many wonderful artists lived and worked in these city-states. The Italian artists Leonardo da Vinci and Michelangelo were two of the world's greatest painters.

From the 1500's to 1800's, France, Spain, and Austria controlled most of Italy. In 1861, most of Italy was joined together under one Italian king.

In 1922, Benito Mussolini became the prime minister, or leader, of Italy. He became very powerful. By 1925, he completely controlled the country. He was a strong leader but sometimes cruel. Italy and Germany were partners during World War II (1939–1945). They lost the war. In 1945, Mussolini lost his power and was killed by a group of Italians. Soon after the war, Italy became a republic. Today the people of Italy vote to decide who their leaders will be.

Other articles to read: **Alps; Leaning Tower of Pisa; Leonardo da Vinci; Michelangelo; Mount Etna; Pompeii; Rome; Venice; Vesuvius.**

Ivory

A Japanese ivory netsuke was worn on a cord around the waist.

Ivory is a hard material that makes up the tusks and teeth of certain animals. The tusks of the African elephant are actually long, curved upper teeth. They are the most common source of ivory. Other ivory comes from the tusks of the walrus and the narwhal—a kind of whale—and from the teeth of the hippopotamus and the sperm whale.

Ivory has been carved into objects and works of art for thousands of years. It has also been used to make piano keys. It comes in different colors, from white to pale pink, yellow, or tan.

In 1989, all trade in ivory was banned. Too many elephants were being killed for their tusks. Today, some countries are allowed to sell small amounts of ivory.

A carved ivory horse from prehistoric times.

These ivory hinged plaques were carved around A.D. 500.

Ivory Coast

• •

Ivory Coast is a country in western Africa. It lies on the Gulf of Guinea, where Africa sticks out into the Atlantic Ocean. It is bordered by Burkina Faso, Ghana, Guinea, Liberia, and Mali. Ivory Coast got its name in the late 1400's, when French sailors began to trade for ivory there. The country's name in French, the official language, is Côte d'Ivoire. Yamoussoukro is the capital. Abidjan is the country's largest city and main port.

Ivory Coast has several kinds of land. The eastern part of the coast is flat and sandy. The western part of the coast has small, rocky cliffs. A tropical forest lies beyond the coastal strip. In the north, the forest changes to savanna, grassland with scattered trees.

Nearly all of Ivory Coast's people are Africans. Most of them are farmers who live in small villages. Farmers grow the country's main products, coffee and cacao (*kuh KAY oh*). Cacao seeds are used to make chocolate. Most Ivorians live in homes that have dried mud walls and straw or metal roofs.

Long ago, great African kingdoms existed in what is now Ivory Coast. The region became a French colony in 1893, and France made it part of French West Africa in 1895. In 1960, Ivory Coast became independent, free from French control.

Facts About Ivory Coast

Capital: Yamoussoukro.

Area: 124,504 sq. mi. (322,463 km²).

Population: Estimated 1998 population— 15,684,000.

Official language: French.

Climate: Hot and rainy along the coast, hotter and less humid inland.

Chief products:

Agriculture and forestry: bananas, cacao, cassava, coffee, corn, palm oil, pineapples, rice, timber, yams.

Manufacturing: cloth, processed foods, refined petroleum products, timber products.

Form of government: Republic.

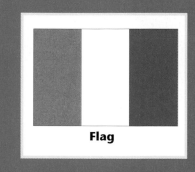

Flag

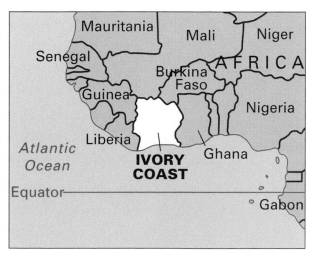

Ivory Coast and its neighbors

Jj

is the tenth letter of the English alphabet.

Special ways of expressing the letter J

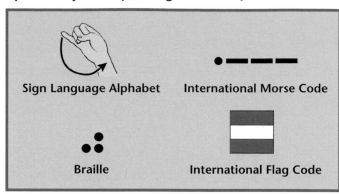

Sign Language Alphabet

International Morse Code

Braille

International Flag Code

Development of the letter J

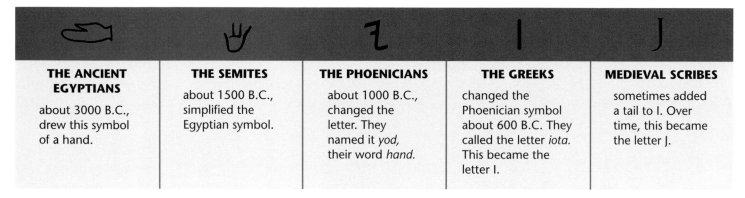

THE ANCIENT EGYPTIANS	THE SEMITES	THE PHOENICIANS	THE GREEKS	MEDIEVAL SCRIBES
about 3000 B.C., drew this symbol of a hand.	about 1500 B.C., simplified the Egyptian symbol.	about 1000 B.C., changed the letter. They named it *yod*, their word *hand*.	changed the Phoenician symbol about 600 B.C. They called the letter *iota*. This became the letter I.	sometimes added a tail to I. Over time, this became the letter J.

Andrew Jackson

Jackson, Andrew

Andrew Jackson (1767-1845) became the seventh president of the United States in 1829. He served from 1829 to 1837. He was the first U.S. president born in a log cabin.

Andrew Jackson was born on March 15, 1767, along the border between North and South Carolina. His family was poor. His father died before he was born, and his mother died when he was 14 years old.

Jackson became a lawyer in 1787. He worked as a government lawyer in Tennessee and served in the volunteer army. In the War of 1812, he helped the city of New Orleans, Louisiana, fight the British. The British were defeated.

In 1824, Jackson wanted to be the Democratic-Republican Party's candidate for president. But his party chose John Quincy Adams. In 1828, Jackson ran for president and won. As president, he got rid of the Bank of the United States, even though the bank had supporters in Congress. Jackson thought the bank was not handling the nation's money properly.

In 1832, Jackson ran for president again. He won easily. He was the only president to see the national debt paid off.

Several states wanted to take over lands that belonged to American Indian tribes. Jackson would not stop the states, and Congress passed a law ordering the tribes to move. Thousands of Indians had to leave their homes and move west. Many Indians died on the way.

After his second term, Jackson returned to Tennessee. He remained interested in politics until he died.

As a teenager, Jackson was a Revolutionary War soldier and was captured. Jackson was slashed with a sword for refusing to clean a British soldier's boots.

Jesse Jackson, *left,* meets with U.S. Secretary of State Madeleine Albright and President Bill Clinton.

Jackson, Jesse Louis

Jesse Louis Jackson (1941-   ) is an American political leader. He is active in civil rights. Many people wanted him to run for president of the United States in 1984 and 1988. He was not elected president, but he became famous as a speaker.

Jackson was born in Greenville, South Carolina. He became a Baptist minister and worked for organizations that tried to get jobs, business, and voting power for African Americans. These organizations included Operation Breadbasket, which he ran from 1966 to 1971, People United to Serve Humanity (PUSH), which he set up in 1971, and the Rainbow Coalition (*KOH uh LIHSH uhn*), which he started in 1984.

Jackson also worked to free political prisoners in other countries. He received the 1989 Spingarn Medal, an important award given to outstanding African Americans.

Jade

Jade (*jayd*) is a valuable stone with beautiful colors. It is known for its strength and hardness. The Chinese have used jade for fine carvings and jewelry for more than 3,000 years.

Today, most jade comes from New Zealand. However, a rare and valuable kind of jade is found in Burma, Japan, and California. Jade is usually white or green, but it can be dark green, yellow, red, gray, or black. One rare type of jade is clear, like glass.

Two minerals, jadeite and nephrite, have been called jade. Both minerals are made of very fine needles. These needles are woven tightly together. That is what makes jade good for carving. It can be cut thin and carved with delicate patterns. Today, most jade is carved in China.

Jewelry carved from ivory (white) and jade (dark)

Jaguar

Jaguars (*JAG wahrz*) are the largest, strongest wild cats of North and South America. They live in the Southwestern United States, Mexico, and Central and South America.

Jaguars live in forests, grasslands, and shrubby areas. They hunt many kinds of animals, including deer, fish, turtles, and wild pigs. Jaguars grow up to $8\frac{1}{2}$ feet (2.6 meters) long, including the tail. Their fur is golden or brownish-yellow with many spots.

Female jaguars have two to four young, which each weigh about 2 pounds (0.9 kilograms) at birth. They hunt with their mother for two years.

In some areas, very few jaguars are left. Selling jaguars or their skins is against the law in the United States.

Jaguar

Jail. See Prison.

Jakarta

Jakarta (*juh KAHR tuh*) is the capital city of Indonesia, a country in Southeast Asia. Jakarta is also Indonesia's main business center and its largest city. Nearly 7 million people live there.

Near the center of Jakarta is Medan Merdeka, or Freedom Square. Around it are many modern hotels, offices, and government buildings. Jakarta has a museum and a center that features art, music, theater, and a planetarium. Jakarta's sports stadium holds 200,000 people.

People have lived in what is now Jakarta for more than 1,500 years. The Dutch took control of the area in 1619. They named the city Batavia. In 1949, when Indonesia became independent from the Netherlands, its name was changed to Jakarta.

Jakarta is Indonesia's main business center.

Jamaica

●●●

Facts About Jamaica

Capital: Kingston.

Area: 4,243 sq. mi. (10,990 km²).

Population: Estimated 1998 population—2,504,000.

Official language: English.

Climate: Hot and wet.

Chief products:

Agriculture: bananas, cacao, citrus fruits, coconuts, coffee, sugar cane.

Manufacturing and processing: alumina, cement, chemicals, clothing, machinery, petroleum products, rum, sugar.

Mining: bauxite, gypsum.

Form of government: Constitutional monarchy. Jamaica's people elect their leaders, but the country's head is the British king or queen.

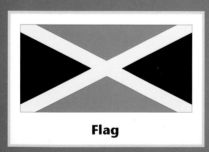

Flag

Jamaica (*juh MAY kuh*) is a small island nation in the West Indies. It lies south of Cuba in the Caribbean Sea. It is the third largest island in the Caribbean Sea. Kingston is the capital and largest city of Jamaica.

Close to a million people visit Jamaica each year. They come for the island's pleasant weather and beautiful beaches and mountains.

Jamaica is part of a group of islands called the Greater Antilles. The island has three land regions: coastal plains, central hills and highlands, and eastern mountains.

Most of Jamaica's people have a black African or mixed black African and European (Afro-European) background. Other groups in the country include Chinese, Indians, Europeans, and Syrians. English is the official language. However, many of the people speak their own form of English. It is different from the English spoken by Americans and English people.

Many of Jamaica's people work on farms. Sugar is the most important crop. Jamaica is among the world's leading producers of bauxite. Bauxite is the material from which aluminum is made. Much of Jamaica's money comes from the many people who visit each year.

Arawak Indians lived in Jamaica when Christopher Columbus arrived there in 1494. The Spaniards controlled Jamaica until the mid-1600's, when the British took over. Jamaica became independent in 1962.

Other articles to read: **Caribbean Sea.**

Jamaica and its neighbors

Japan

Japan is an island country in the North Pacific Ocean. It lies off the east coast of Asia, across from Russia, Korea, and China. Four large islands and thousands of smaller ones make up Japan. Tokyo is Japan's capital and largest city.

Land. Japan is a land of great beauty. Mountains and hills cover most of the country. The Japanese islands are made up of the rugged upper part of a great mountain range that rises from the floor of the North Pacific Ocean.

Japan suffers from many earthquakes. The Japanese islands have about 1,500 earthquakes a year. Most of them are small, but severe earthquakes strike Japan every few years. Undersea quakes sometimes cause huge waves, called tsunami (*tsoo NAH mee*), along the coast of the Pacific Ocean. These waves can cause great damage. The Japanese islands also have more than 60 volcanoes that could erupt at any time.

The four main islands, from largest to smallest, are Honshu, Hokkaido, Kyushu, and Shikoku. Thousands of smaller islands lie near these islands. Japan's land also includes the Ryukyu and Bonin island chains.

A Japanese home

Facts About Japan

Capital: Tokyo.

Area: 145,870 sq. mi. (377,801 km²).

Population: Estimated 1998 population—125,922,000.

Official language: Japanese.

Climate: Central and southern Japan have hot summers, mild winters, and little rain or snow. Hokkaido, northern Honshu, and high mountain areas are colder.

Chief products:

Agriculture: cabbage, Chinese cabbage, hogs, mandarin oranges, milk, potatoes, poultry and eggs, rice, strawberries, tea, white radishes.

Fishing: clams, eels, mackerel, oysters, pollock, salmon, sardines, scallops, squid, tuna.

Manufacturing: automobiles, cameras, cement, chemicals, cloth, computers, iron and steel, paper and newsprint, processed foods, television sets, tires, watches.

Mining: coal.

Form of government: Japan's people elect their leaders, who serve in a parliament. The country is headed by an emperor.

Flag

Honshu is Japan's largest island. Most of the Japanese people live on this island. Japan's tallest and most famous peak, Mount Fuji, or Fujiyama, rises on Honshu. It is a volcano, but it is no longer active, which means it does not erupt.

Hokkaido is Japan's second largest island. Many of the people of Hokkaido work in dairy farming, fishing, and forestry. Many people visit the island for fun and relaxation.

Kyushu is the southernmost of Japan's main islands. After Honshu, Kyushu has the most people. Parts of Kyushu have many volcanoes.

Shikoku is the smallest of the main Japanese islands. Most of the people of this island live in the north. Farmers grow rice and different kinds of fruits along the Inland Sea there.

The Ryukyu and Bonin islands belonged to Japan until after World War II (1939-1945), when the United States took control of them. The United States has since returned the islands to Japan.

Japan and its neighbors

People. Japan has one of the largest populations in the world. The Japanese people come from groups of people who came to the islands from other parts of Asia. No one knows for sure when people first arrived in Japan, but it was more than 30,000 years ago. Some historians think that a group of people in Japan called the Ainu may come from the original settlers of the Japanese islands. Today most Ainu live on Hokkaido. Some Chinese and Koreans also live in Japan.

Resources and products. Japan is one of the world's richest countries, even though it has few natural resources. Japan earns most of its money from the many things it makes and sells. The Japanese make such things as cars, computers, steel, TV sets, and tires. Japan's factories have some of the best equipment in the world. Japan buys many of the materials needed to make these products from other countries. Then it sells these products—for example, cars—to other countries.

Building is also a big business in Japan. This business grew quickly after World War II, when so much rebuilding was needed. Many of Japan's cities were destroyed during the war. Today, Japanese companies build hotels and office buildings throughout the world.

Throughout most of Japan's history, farming was its main business. As late as 1950, almost half of Japan's workers worked on farms. But as Japan's other companies grew, farming became less important. Japan is one of the most important fishing nations in the world today.

The Shitennoti Temple in Osaka, Japan

History. The early people of Japan borrowed many Chinese ideas about how to organize society and government. More than 1,000 years ago, warriors called samuri (*SAM uh ry*) became important in Japan. The head of the government was the emperor. But from the 1100's to the mid-1800's, real power was in the hands of a military leader called the shogun (*SHO guhn*).

During the mid-1500's, the first Europeans arrived in Japan. Trade began with several European countries. During the early 1600's, however, the rulers of Japan decided to cut the country off almost entirely from the rest of the world. This lasted until 1853, when Commodore Matthew C. Perry of the United States sailed his warships into Tokyo Bay. A few years later, Japan agreed to trade with the United States.

During the 1870's, the Japanese government began to work toward making the country more modern. New ideas and ways of making things were brought in from other countries. By the early 1900's, Japan had become a great business leader and military power.

During the 1930's, Japan's military leaders gained control of the government. On December 7, 1941, Japan attacked the United States at Pearl Harbor in Hawaii. This brought the United States into World War II (1939-1945). In August 1945, the United States dropped the first atomic bomb ever used in a war on the Japanese city of Hiroshima. It dropped an atomic bomb on Nagasaki two days later. On September 2, 1945, Japan gave up, and World War II ended.

After World War II, other countries controlled Japan. Many Japanese cities and businesses had been destroyed during the war. The Japanese people worked hard to get over the effects of the war and, by the 1970's, Japan was doing well again. Today, the country is very successful.

Other articles to read: **Kyoto; Mount Fuji; Osaka; Shinto; Tokyo.**

Japanese Sumo wrestlers parade around the ring before a match.

Jazz

●●●●●●●●●●●●●●●●●●●●●●●●●●●

Jazz is a kind of music that began in the United States in the late 1800's. The music grew from a mixture of different kinds of music, including black American music and African rhythms.

Count Basie and his orchestra were jazz stars during the "swing" era.

Jazz musicians often make up music as they play it. Musicians call this improvisation (*ihm pruh vy ZAY shuhn*). Improvisation is part of what makes jazz different from other kinds of music. It makes the person who plays the music the person who creates it. Another important part of jazz is called syncopation (*sihng kuh PAY shuhn*). In syncopation, the musical patterns are uneven and the musical notes are accented, or stressed, in unusual places.

Instruments

Jazz may be performed by a single musician or by a small group of musicians called a combo. Sometimes it is performed by a band of 10 or more musicians. Many instruments are used to play jazz. Brass instruments used to play jazz include the trumpet and the slide trombone. Reed instruments include the clarinet and saxophone. Other instruments include the piano, drums, and bass. Guitar is also used in some types of jazz.

Today, jazz remains popular with amateur musicians such as this high school band.

History of jazz

The earliest jazz was performed by African Americans who had not gone to music school. They listened to ragtime, a type of music that has great energy and syncopation. They also listened to the blues, a sad kind of music with much

Many jazz performers, such as Marian McPartland, *above*, play the piano.

Jelly Roll Morton, *at the piano,* was the first important jazz pianist and the first great jazz composer.

repetition. They listened to band music played at African American funerals and in parades. And they knew many folk songs and pieces of dance music. From all these types of music, jazz was born. Jazz probably started in New Orleans in the early 1900's. Today, this style of jazz music is called Dixieland Jazz.

In time, other types of jazz came about. The 1920's is often called the golden age of jazz or the jazz age. Jazz spread from New Orleans to other cities, such as Memphis, St. Louis, Kansas City, Chicago, Detroit, and New York City. It began to be played on the radio. Jazz stayed popular after this golden age. In the 1930's, big bands formed with both black and white musicians. Jazz singers sang popular songs. Many ordinary people, both black and white, enjoyed the bands and the singers and danced to the music.

Swing jazz was popular with the big bands of the 1930's. It had its own special rhythm. The name "swing" came from the song "It Don't Mean a Thing If It Ain't Got That Swing," which was recorded in 1932 by Duke Ellington.

In the 1940's, bebop was a new jazz style. It was a difficult style, and the musicians who played it had great skill. Each phrase, or part, of the music had many notes and many surprises. Cool jazz, popular in the 1940's and 1950's, had a soft sound. Hard bop, in the 1950's, added blues music and church music to jazz.

In the 1970's, fusion jazz became popular. It combined jazz with rock music. Some jazz musicians used electronic instruments, and some even used computers to create new sounds.

Today, many styles of jazz are popular. Many musicians play swing and bebop. Others play fusion jazz. Electronic technology is also being used more in jazz music today.

Other articles to read: **Armstrong, Louis; Blues; Brass instruments; Ellington, Duke; Fitzgerald, Ella; Guitar; Piano.**

Jefferson, Thomas

● ●

Thomas Jefferson (1743-1826) served as the third president of the United States from 1801 to 1809. Before becoming president, Jefferson was vice president to John Adams and held many other government offices, including governor of Virginia. He is best remembered for writing the Declaration of Independence in 1776. The Declaration of Independence announced that the 13 American colonies were free from British control.

Jefferson had many interests and great talents. He designed buildings, including his own home, called Monticello. He loved art, music, and reading. In addition, he was an inventor. He invented a plow, a lap desk, and a machine that could figure out codes.

He thought and wrote about politics and government. He believed that most people could govern, or rule, themselves without much government control. He also believed in freedom of religion and freedom of speech, including ideas printed in newspapers.

During Jefferson's time as president, he almost doubled the size of the United States. He did this in 1803 with the Louisiana Purchase. He agreed to buy a huge area of land from France. That land was called the Louisiana Territory. It stretched from the Mississippi River to the Rocky Mountains.

After he left the presidency, Jefferson continued to work for the American people. He advised the presidents who followed him, James Madison and James Monroe. He also started the University of Virginia. He was proud of this school, saying that it was based on the "freedom of the human mind to explore."

Other articles to read: **Declaration of Independence; Louisiana Purchase.**

Thomas Jefferson

Monticello, Thomas Jefferson's home in Virginia

Jellyfish

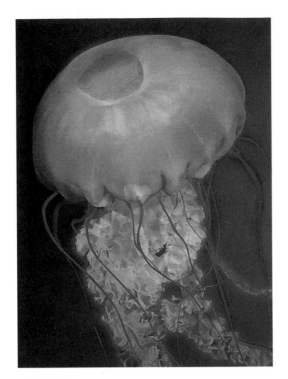

Jellyfish

Jellyfish are sea animals. They are filled with a jellylike material that helps them hold their shape and float. Some kinds of jellyfish are as small as a pea. Others are as much as 7 feet (2.1 meters) across.

The body of a jellyfish is umbrella-shaped. A tube with a mouth and four short arms hangs down underneath it. Long tentacles dangle around the edges of the body. The tentacles have stinging cells.

Jellyfish swim by opening the body like an umbrella and then quickly shutting it. This movement squeezes out water and makes them shoot upward. When they stop moving, they sink slowly. As they sink, they catch small animals, sting them, and swallow them.

Some jellyfish are very dangerous. Their sting can be painful or even poisonous to people.

Jemison, Mae Carol

Mae Carol Jemison (1956-   ) is an American doctor who became an astronaut. She was the first African American woman to travel in space.

Jemison was born in Decatur, Alabama. She grew up in Chicago and studied medicine at Cornell University in New York. For two years, she worked for the Peace Corps in Africa.

In September 1992, Jemison flew on the spacecraft Endeavour. She spent eight days in space. While on the Endeavour, she performed many scientific experiments.

Jemison left the space program in March 1993. She went to work on other projects, including the improvement of health care in western Africa.

Mae Carol Jemison

Jerusalem

● ●

Jerusalem is the capital and largest city of Israel. People have lived in Jerusalem for thousands of years.

For many years, Jerusalem has been a religious center to Jews, Christians, and Muslims. Jews think of Jerusalem as a holy city because it was their center of activity during the times of the Bible. Christians think of Jerusalem as holy because many events in the life of Jesus Christ took place there. Muslims think of the city as holy because they believe that their prophet, Muhammad, rose to heaven from the city.

In 1948, Jerusalem was divided between Israel and Jordan. Jordan is a neighboring country of Israel. Israel held West Jerusalem. Jordan controlled East Jerusalem. Israel captured East Jerusalem in the Arab-Israeli war of 1967 and gave its people the same rights as other Israelis. West Jerusalem is the modern part of the city. East Jerusalem includes the walled Old City, a part of the city that dates back to the times of the Bible.

The Western Wall of the Jewish holy temple destroyed by the Romans in A.D. 70 still stands in Jerusalem. Jews come from around the world to pray at this most holy site and insert messages in its crevices.

Today, most of Jerusalem's people are Jews. The rest are Muslims and Christians. Jerusalem is a city of three Sabbaths—Friday for Muslims, Saturday for Jews, and Sunday for Christians. The Sabbath is the day of the week on which the faithful rest from work and gather for worship. Businesses in Jerusalem may be closed on any of these days.

Jesus Christ

● ●

Jesus Christ was one of the world's greatest religious leaders. The Christian religion was founded on His life and teachings. Most Christians believe that He is the Son of God sent to Earth to save all people. Even many people who are not Christians believe that He was a great and wise teacher.

Four books of the New Testament tell almost all we know of Jesus. These are the Gospels of Matthew, Mark, Luke, and John. The day of Jesus's birth was first celebrated on December 25 in the early 300's. Mary was the mother of Jesus. Joseph was Mary's husband.

Jesus's mission, or work on Earth, was to tell the world that the Kingdom of God was coming. The "Kingdom of God" meant that God was going to change the way of life on Earth.

Jesus's announcement was good news for many people. But rulers and religious leaders were unhappy with Him. They were afraid of Him. They captured Him and took Him to Pontius Pilate, the Roman governor of Judea. Pilate sentenced Jesus to die by being nailed to a cross.

According to the Bible, Jesus arose from His grave shortly after His death. He then stayed on Earth during the next 40 days and taught His followers. Then He rose into heaven.

Other articles to read: **Christianity; Christmas; Easter.**

Jesus taught His wisdom to His close followers. They became known as His apostles.

Jet. See Airplane.

Jews

● ●

Jews are people who came from an ancient people called the Hebrews. The Hebrews were established by a shepherd named Abraham, between 3,500 and 3,800 years ago. Abraham settled in what is now Israel, where he established the Hebrews. Over a period of hundreds of years, Jews moved to different places throughout the world.

The Jews have been important people in world history. They made the Hebrew Bible. The Hebrew Bible, with its belief in one God, became an important part of three world religions—Judaism, Christianity, and Islam.

Jewish history has been full of sad events. The Jews made up a very small group almost everywhere they went to live, and they often were treated cruelly. In Europe, during World War II (1939-1945), about 6 million Jews were killed in the Holocaust. The Holocaust was the planned murder of Jewish people by the German government of that time, which was known as the Nazi government.

Beginning in the late 1800's, many Jews from Eastern Europe moved to Israel. At that time, Israel was called Palestine. Many more Jews came to Palestine after the Holocaust. The nation of Israel was founded in 1948.

There are about 13 million Jews in the world today. The United States is home to the largest number of Jews. About 6 million Jews live in the United States. About $4\frac{1}{2}$ million Jews live in Israel. Other countries with large numbers of Jews include France, Russia, the United Kingdom, Canada, and Argentina.

Other articles to read: **Abraham; Hanukkah; Holocaust; Israel; Judaism; Passover; Pentateuch; Rosh Ha-Shanah; Yom Kippur.**

Jews pray at the Western Wall, which also is called the Wailing Wall. This holy site is all that is left of the Jews' holy temple in Jerusalem from the time of the Bible.

Joan of Arc, Saint

Joan of Arc

Saint Joan of Arc (1412?-1431) was a French hero. She became a saint of the Roman Catholic Church.

Joan of Arc, or Jeanne d'Arc (*zhahn dahrk*), was born at Domrémy in France. By the time she was 13, she had seen religious visions and heard strange voices. Joan believed these voices came from saints. The voices said God had chosen her to help King Charles VII of France force the English out of France.

When Joan was 17, she went to see the king. Charles gave her soldiers to command. In April 1429, she set out to rescue the city of Orléans from the English. In 10 days, her soldiers saved the city.

Charles had never been crowned king. Joan led Charles and his followers safely to Reims, France, where Charles was crowned on July 17, 1429.

Charles allowed Joan to try to free Paris. In May 1430, she was captured by French people called Burgundians, who supported the English. The Burgundians handed her over to the English for a large amount of money. She was tried for witchcraft and for not believing in the accepted religion. Joan said that the voices she heard had come from God, and she would not change her mind. She was sentenced to death.

Joan was tied to a wooden post and burned to death in Rouen, France on May 30, 1431. In 1455, her family asked for a new trial. In 1456, the pope said she was innocent. Joan of Arc was made a saint in 1920. May 30 is her feast day.

Job

● ●

Job (*johb*) was a religious and good man who was made to suffer. His story is told in the Bible, in the Book of Job.

The Bible tells that God allowed the Devil to test Job's faith. The Devil made many terrible things happen to Job. His friends thought Job was being punished for wrongdoing. But Job said he had done no wrong. His friends said that he should be sorry and ask for forgiveness. But Job kept saying that he had done no wrong.

Then God appeared to Job. Job realized that he was nothing compared to God. He accepted God's judgment of him, even though he could not understand it. In the end, God made him rich again.

Job. See **Career.**

Job suffered greatly in the Bible story.

Johannesburg is South Africa's largest city.

Johannesburg

Johannesburg (*joh HAN ihs BURG*) is a city in South Africa. It has more than 700,000 people. With its surrounding suburbs, it has nearly 2 million people, making it South Africa's largest city.

Johannesburg is in the northeastern part of South Africa. It stands on the world's richest gold field. Deep gold mines tunnel through the earth beneath the city. The area also is rich in coal, iron, and other minerals.

Johannesburg was founded, or started, in 1886. Today, it is an important business and transportation center. It has two universities. It also has an art gallery and museums. Music, theater, and ballet companies perform at its Civic Center.

Johnson, Andrew

Andrew Johnson (1808-1875) became the seventeenth president of the United States in 1865, after President Abraham Lincoln was shot.

Johnson was born in Raleigh, North Carolina, on December 29, 1808. He became a tailor and settled in Greeneville, Tennessee. His wife taught him to write and do arithmetic. He built a good business, became the mayor, and was elected to the state government in 1835. He was elected to Congress in 1843.

Abraham Lincoln was elected president in 1860. In 1861, the Civil War (1861-1865) began. The Southern States seceded (*seh SEED uhd*) from, or left, the nation.

Lincoln was elected again in 1864, with Johnson as his vice president. On April 14, 1865, only five days after the war ended, President

Andrew Johnson

Lincoln was shot. Lincoln died the next day, and Johnson became president.

When the war ended, Congress could not agree on how to treat the Southern States. Some felt the South should be treated harshly. Johnson did not agree. Soon Congress and Johnson were fighting over laws that Congress passed. On February 24, 1868, the United States House of Representatives voted to impeach (*ihm PEECH*) Johnson, or accuse him of crimes. The trial was held in the Senate. A two-thirds vote was needed to find him guilty. He was found not guilty by one vote.

After the trial, Johnson finished his term and went back to Tennessee. In 1875, he was elected to the U.S. Senate. Many senators welcomed him back. He died a few months later.

Johnson, Earvin "Magic"
● ●

Earvin "Magic" Johnson (1959-   ) is one of the greatest players in basketball history. He played guard for the Los Angeles Lakers of the National Basketball Association (NBA).

Earvin Johnson, Jr., was born in Lansing, Michigan. He went to Michigan State University. In 1979, his team won the National Collegiate Athletic Association (NCAA) tournament, the national college championship.

Johnson joined the Lakers in 1979. He helped that team win five NBA championships, and he won the Most Valuable Player award twice.

In the 1991-1992 season, Johnson learned that he had HIV, the virus that causes AIDS. He retired from basketball. However, he played on the United States "Dream Team" in the 1992 Summer Olympics. The team won a gold medal. Johnson returned to the Lakers for a short time in 1996.

Earvin "Magic" Johnson

Johnson, Lyndon Baines

Lyndon Baines Johnson

Lyndon Baines Johnson (1908-1973) became the 36th president of the United States in 1963 after President John F. Kennedy was murdered.

Lyndon Johnson was born on August 27, 1908, near Stonewall, Texas. He became a high school teacher. In 1931, he worked to get Richard Kleberg, a local Democrat, elected to Congress. Kleberg won and took Johnson to Washington, D.C., as his secretary.

Johnson ran for Congress in 1937 and won. During World War II (1939-1945), he served in the U.S. Navy. After the war, he returned to Congress.

Johnson was skillful at getting laws passed and soon became a Democratic leader. In 1960, John F. Kennedy was elected president and Johnson became vice president.

On November 22, 1963, President Kennedy was shot in Dallas, Texas. Johnson became president when Kennedy died. In 1964, Johnson ran for president and won.

Johnson asked people to work toward the Great Society. He wanted to improve education, help poor people, and help the cities. But the Vietnam War, which began in 1957 and involved U.S. troops, was getting worse. Some people felt U.S. soldiers should leave Vietnam. Others felt the United States should send more troops to end the war.

In March 1968, Johnson said he would not run for president again. Richard M. Nixon, a Republican, was elected in November. After Nixon took office, Johnson retired to his ranch in Texas.

Johnson is sworn in as president of the United States, watched by Jacqueline Kennedy, right, the widow of President Kennedy.

Jones, John Paul

John Paul Jones (1747-1792) is often called the *Father of the American Navy.* When the British asked him to surrender in battle, he replied, "I have not yet begun to fight."

Jones was born in Scotland. His name was John Paul. He went to sea when he was 12 years old. In 1769, he was put in charge of a ship. A few years later, he was accused of killing one of his crew. He fled to America and added Jones to his name.

When the Revolutionary War started in 1775, Jones went back to sea. He commanded many ships. In one attack, his ship was so close to a British ship that their guns touched. The sailors on the two ships fought hand to hand. After three hours, the British surrendered.

A few years after the war ended, Jones served in the Russian navy. In 1789, he moved to Paris.

John Paul Jones

Joplin, Scott

Scott Joplin (1868-1917) was an American musician who wrote lively music called ragtime.

Joplin was born in Texarkana, Texas. About 1894, he settled in Sedalia, Missouri. He played piano at the Maple Leaf Club. The owner of a music store published Joplin's "Maple Leaf Rag" (1899) and many other pieces.

In 1907, Joplin moved to New York City. He had written an opera, *Treemonisha,* and other works for the stage. He wanted to get them performed. He did not succeed. Joplin died in a mental hospital.

In the 1970's, people began to play Joplin's music again. His music was used in *The Sting,* a popular movie, and *Treemonisha* was performed. In 1976, the Pulitzer Prize officials gave Joplin a special award for his contribution to American music.

Scott Joplin

Jordan

● ●

Facts About Jordan

Capital: Amman.

Area: 35,475 sq. mi. (91,880 km²).

Population: Estimated 1998 population— 4,480,000.

Official language: Arabic.

Climate: Hot and dry in Jordan River Valley and Syrian Desert. Milder and wetter on the plateau.

Chief products:

Agriculture: barley, cabbages, citrus fruits, cucumbers, eggplants, grapes, melons, olives, tomatoes, wheat.

Manufacturing: batteries, cement, ceramics, cloth, detergents, fertilizer, medicines, petroleum products, shoes.

Mining: phosphate, potash.

Form of government: Constitutional monarchy.

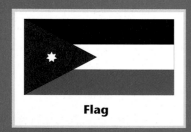

Flag

Jordan is a country in southwestern Asia, in the region known as the Middle East. It lies on the East Bank of the Jordan River. The country is bordered by Iraq, Israel, Saudi Arabia, Syria, and the West Bank, an area of land west of the Jordan River. Amman is Jordan's capital and largest city.

Land. Jordan's land includes deserts, mountains, deep valleys, and rolling plains. The country has a warm, pleasant climate, but some parts get very little rain.

Jordan's largest cities and most of the country's farmland are on the Transjordan Plateau (*plah TOH*), an area of high flat land in western Jordan.

People. Most of the people of Jordan are Jordanian Arabs, people who speak the Arabic language and whose ancestors were from Jordan. The rest of the people are mainly Palestinian Arabs. They or their familes came to Jordan to escape the Arab-Israeli wars of 1948 and 1967. Other Palestinians moved from the West Bank to Amman between the wars, when the West Bank was part of Jordan.

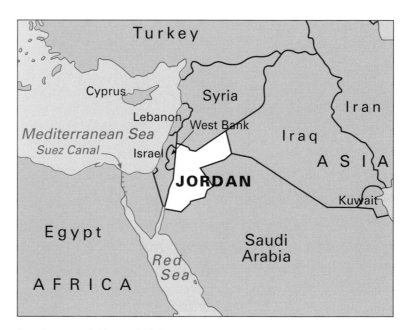

Jordan and its neighbors

Most of the people of Jordan follow the religion of Islam. A few are Christians.

Many Jordanians work in hotels, restaurants, and banks. Others have jobs in government and the military. Some people work in factories in Amman. Many Jordanians work in oil-producing Arab countries. These workers send money to their families in Jordan.

Resources and products. Most of Jordan's money comes from such businesses as hotels, restaurants, and banks. Tourism helps support many of the nation's businesses.

Jordan gets some income from factories that make fertilizer and cement. Mines produce phosphates and potash used to make fertilizer.

Amman is Jordan's capital and largest city.

History. The first writings that tell about the area come from about 4,000 years ago. Many groups and empires ruled the land in ancient times, including the Israelites, Egyptians, Assyrians, and Persians. The Romans took control of it just over 2,000 years ago. It was part of the Ottoman Empire from the 1500's to the early 1900's. The Ottoman Empire was based in what is now Turkey.

After World War I (1914-1918), Britain was in charge of what is now Jordan. In the 1920's, Britain let Jordan—then called Transjordan—be partly responsible for its government. Transjordan became independent in 1946. Its name was changed to Jordan in 1949.

From 1948 to 1973, Jordan fought in several wars with Israel. In 1949, Jordan gained control of an area just west of the Jordan River called the West Bank, including part of the city of Jerusalem. Israel captured the West Bank in a war in 1967. Later, Jordan gave up its claim to the West Bank. Jordan and Israel signed a peace treaty in 1994.

Other articles to read: **Dead Sea; Jerusalem; West Bank.**

Jordan, Michael

● ●

Michael Jordan (1963-   ) became one of the most exciting players in the National Basketball Association (NBA). Jordan stands 6 feet 6 inches (198 centimeters) tall. He played guard and forward for the Chicago Bulls in the 1980's and 1990's. His spectacular shooting, especially his leaping shots near the basket, thrilled fans throughout the world. Jordan became one of the highest-scoring players in basketball history.

Michael Jeffrey Jordan was born in New York City and grew up in Wilmington, North Carolina. While he was a freshman at the University of North Carolina, he made the winning shot in the championship game of the 1982 National Collegiate Athletic Association (NCAA) basketball tournament. He joined the Bulls in 1984. In the 1984-85 NBA season, Jordan scored 2,313 points, more than any other player that season. He was named Rookie of the Year. A rookie is a new player. Jordan played on the United States teams that won first place in men's basketball at the 1984 and 1992 Summer Olympic Games. He was named the NBA's Most Valuable Player five times between 1987 and 1998. Between 1990 and 1998, Jordan helped lead the Bulls to six NBA championships.

In 1993, Jordan retired from basketball. He decided to play professional baseball. He played minor league baseball as an outfielder for the Chicago White Sox in 1994. He returned to the Bulls in March 1995. Jordan retired from basketball again in 1999.

Michael Jordan powers his way to the hoop.

Joseph, Chief

Chief Joseph (1840?-1904) was a Nez Perce Indian chief. He was famous for leading his people away from battle.

The United States government ordered Joseph's people to move from Oregon to a reservation in Idaho. In June 1877, war broke out between Joseph's people and the U.S. Army. Joseph's people won several battles. But Joseph knew they could not defeat the Army. He led his people toward Canada, hoping to join with Sioux Indians there.

Joseph led his people for more than 1,000 miles (1,600 kilometers), fighting off Army troops along the way. Finally, not far from the Canadian border, he surrendered, or gave up. The United States government then sent Joseph and his people to the Indian Territory in Oklahoma. Joseph later lived on a reservation in Washington state.

Chief Joseph, leader of the Nez Perce Indians

Judaism

Judaism (*JOO dee ihz uhm*) is the religion of the Jewish people. Judaism is the world's oldest major religion.

The most important teaching of Judaism is that there is one God. Judaism teaches that God wants people to do what is right and to be fair and kind to other people. Many Jewish people believe that someday God will send a special person, called a Messiah (*muh SY uh*), to Earth. The Messiah will bring the Jews together, lead them in God's way, and defeat their enemies.

The Jewish Sabbath, or day of worship, begins at sundown every Friday and ends at nightfall on Saturday. On the Sabbath, many Jewish people attend services and have special meals at home. Important holy days and festivals of Judaism

The Star of David is the symbol of Judaism.

A boy reads from the Torah at his Bar Mitzvah, the Jewish coming-of-age ceremony.

include Rosh Ha-Shanah, Yom Kippur, Passover, and Hanukkah.

The synagogue is the Jewish house of worship. It is also a center for Jewish education and social activities. A rabbi is a Jewish leader and teacher. A cantor chants the prayers during worship in the synagogue.

The teachings of Judaism are described in two important collections of writings—the Hebrew Bible and the Talmud. The Hebrew Bible is what Christians call the Old Testament. The first five books of the Hebrew Bible make up the Torah. The Torah is the most important of all Jewish holy writings. It contains the basic laws of Judaism and tells about the history of the Jews. The Talmud is a guide to the laws that Jewish people are supposed to live by.

Other articles to read: **Abraham; Hanukkah; Holocaust; Israel; Jews; Passover; Pentateuch; Rosh Ha-Shanah; Yom Kippur.**

Judo. See Martial arts.

Julian, Percy

Percy Julian (*PUR see JOOL yuhn*) (1899-1975) was a famous American scientist. He was a chemist (*KEHM ihst*), a scientist who studies substances and how they change.

Julian created a drug used to treat an eye disease called glaucoma (*glah KOH muh*). He also found a way to make a drug called cortisone (*KAWR tuh zohn*). Cortisone is made naturally in the human body. With Julian's method, cortisone could be made from chemicals at low cost. Doctors use cortisone to treat eye and skin disorders, some kinds of cancer, and other diseases.

Julian was born in Montgomery, Alabama. He graduated from DePauw University and got a

Percy Julian

master's degree from Harvard University. Then he earned a Ph.D. degree from the University of Vienna, Austria.

Julian created more than 100 new chemical products. Many of them were made from soybeans. One product was a fire-fighting liquid that saved many lives during World War II (1939-1945).

In 1953, Julian founded, or started, Julian Laboratories. The business had branches in Mexico and South America. In 1964, he became the head of the Julian Research Institute. The institute does research on chemicals made from soybeans.

Jump rope

Jump rope is a game and a sport. It is also good exercise. People can jump rope by themselves or with others. Sometimes they do tricks and say rhymes while they are jumping.

Jumpers use a piece of medium-weight rope or a jump rope made especially for jumping. A jump rope has handles that let the rope turn easily.

Sometimes jumpers use a long rope. Two people turn the rope while jumpers take turns jumping. In Double Dutch, the turners turn two ropes in opposite directions. The jumpers jump back and forth over both ropes.

Schools and clubs often have jump-rope teams that compete for prizes. People also jump rope for exercise to improve their hearts, lungs, and strength.

Jumping rope is good exercise.

Jungle

Jungles are wild areas that have a thick tangle of tropical plants. Jungles are found in tropical rain forests.

Tropical rain forests have huge trees, long vines, and such animals as parrots and monkeys. In many parts of a rain forest, the trees are so dense, or thick, that sunlight never reaches the ground.

Jungles are the parts of rain forests where sunlight reaches the forest floor. Such jungles grow along rivers and in clearings. Jungles often grow in places where trees have been cut down. Sometimes, people have to cut paths through jungles with long knives called machetes (*muh SHEHT eez*).

Jungles are parts of rain forests where sunlight reaches the forest floor.

Jupiter was the king of gods in Roman myths.

Jupiter

Jupiter was the king of gods in Roman myths (*mihths*), or stories of gods and goddesses. He was a son of Saturn, the ruler of the universe. At first Jupiter was the god of the sky, thunder, and lightning.

Jupiter's wife, Juno, was queen of the gods. Their children included the gods Mars and Vulcan. Many other gods, goddesses, and heroes were Jupiter's children. Some myths say that one goddess, Minerva, sprang full grown from Jupiter's head. Jupiter was also the father of the nine Muses. They were spirits who helped people create art and poetry.

Jupiter's symbols were the oak tree, the eagle, and the thunderbolt. The largest planet is named after him.

Other articles to read: **Mars.**

Jupiter

● ●

Jupiter is the fifth planet from the sun and the largest planet in the solar system. More than 1,000 Earths would fit inside Jupiter. When viewed from Earth, Jupiter appears brighter than most stars. Among the planets, only Venus is brighter. Jupiter is named after the king of the Roman gods.

Jupiter is a giant ball of gas and liquid. It has little or no solid surface. Instead, the planet's surface is made of thick red, brown, yellow, and white clouds. The clouds have dark and light-colored areas. These areas circle the planet and give it a striped appearance.

Jupiter's most outstanding surface feature is the Great Red Spot, a swirling mass of gas. It looks like

Jupiter is the fifth planet from the sun.

Jupiter is a giant ball of gas and liquid.

a TV weather display of a hurricane. The color of the Great Red Spot varies from brick-red to brownish. Jupiter has three thin rings around its middle. They seem to be made mostly of dust particles.

Jupiter rotates, or spins, faster than any other planet. Jupiter's day—that is, the time it takes to spin around once—is only about 10 hours long. By comparison, Earth's day is 24 hours long. Jupiter takes about 12 years to travel once around the sun, while Earth takes one year.

Jupiter has 16 known moons. These moons rotate around Jupiter the way our moon rotates around Earth. Scientists have discovered volcanoes on the moon called Io. They believe that the moon called Europa contains water.

The Great Red Spot of Jupiter is a swirling mass of gas. It looks like a hurricane and is three times as wide as Earth.

The jute plant produces a long, soft, shiny fiber.

Jute is used to make cloth bags, curtains, chair coverings, carpets, burlap, twine, and rope.

Jute

Jute (*joot*) is a long, soft, shiny fiber from the jute plant. It can be woven into rough, strong threads.

Most jute is used to make cloth for wrapping bales, or bundles, of cotton, and to make rough cloth bags called gunny sacks. Jute fibers are also used in curtains, chair coverings, carpets, and coarse cloth called burlap. Jute is used in making twine and rope, too.

Jute grows best in warm, damp areas. China, India, and Bangladesh are the world's biggest growers. Jute fibers are off-white to brown and grow 3 to 15 feet (0.9 to 4.5 meters) long.

K k is the eleventh letter of the English alphabet.

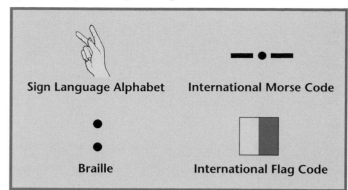

Sign Language Alphabet

International Morse Code

Braille

International Flag Code

Development of the letter K

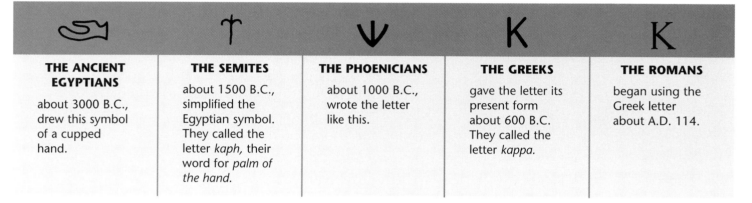

THE ANCIENT EGYPTIANS	THE SEMITES	THE PHOENICIANS	THE GREEKS	THE ROMANS
about 3000 B.C., drew this symbol of a cupped hand.	about 1500 B.C., simplified the Egyptian symbol. They called the letter *kaph*, their word for *palm of the hand*.	about 1000 B.C., wrote the letter like this.	gave the letter its present form about 600 B.C. They called the letter *kappa*.	began using the Greek letter about A.D. 114.

Kabuki

Kabuki (*kah BOO kee*) is a kind of Japanese drama, or play. It has been performed the same way for hundreds of years.

Kabuki plays are popular in Japan. Some of them are about history, and others are about people in everyday life. The scenery is beautiful, and the actors wear colorful costumes and makeup. The acting in kabuki plays is very lively. Chanting and music are part of the plays.

Kabuki began in the 1600's. Some of its style was copied from puppet plays, which were very popular. In kabuki theater, men play all the parts.

Kabuki actors wear colorful costumes and makeup.

Kahlo, Frida

Frida Kahlo (1907-1954) was an important Mexican painter. She was best known for painting pictures of herself that showed her feelings.

Frida Kahlo was born in Coyoacán, a part of Mexico City. When she was 15 years old, she was badly hurt in a bus accident. She had many operations and lost one leg.

Kahlo wanted to be a doctor, but her injuries were too great. She taught herself to paint. In 1929, she married the famous Mexican artist Diego Rivera.

Most of Frida Kahlo's paintings are pictures of herself that show her suffering. She used strong colors and included things that were part of Mexican history. She sometimes painted herself wearing Mexican Indian costumes.

A self-portrait by Frida Kahlo

Kaleidoscope

A kaleidoscope (*kuh LY duh skohp*) is a viewer that shows beautiful colors and designs.

A kaleidoscope has a tube that is closed at both ends. One end has a peephole. The other end has two pieces of glass. A space between them holds bits of colored glass. When you turn the kaleidoscope, the colored bits tumble into different places and form a new design.

Inside the kaleidoscope are two long mirrors. They are slanted in a V shape, and they reach all the way down the tube. The bits of colored glass are reflected in the mirrors. The reflections make the design you see when you look through the peephole.

Other articles to read: **Mirror.**

The mirrors of a kaleidoscope reflect bits of glass in colorful patterns.

Kangaroo

A kangaroo is a type of furry animal that hops on its hind legs. Kangaroos live mainly in central, southern, and eastern Australia.

Kangaroos are mammals. They feed their young with mother's milk. They are a kind of mammal called a marsupial (*mahr SOO pee uhl*). Marsupials give birth to very small babies. Most baby marsupials live in a pocket, or pouch, on the mother's belly until they grow larger.

The two main kinds of kangaroos are red kangaroos and gray kangaroos. A full-grown male kangaroo stands about as tall as a man. Female kangaroos are smaller.

Kangaroos have a small head, a pointed nose, and large ears. They have a long tail and large, powerful hind legs. Kangaroos can hop as fast as 30 miles (48 kilometers) per hour. They use their long tails for balance when they hop.

Kangaroos usually rest in the shade during the day. At night, they feed on grass and small plants. They usually spend their time in small groups.

Female kangaroos give birth to one very tiny baby at a time. The baby is called a joey. A newborn joey is only about 1 inch (2.5 centimeters) long. It fastens itself to a nipple in its mother's pouch and stays there for about six to eight months.

Kangaroos usually live six to eight years. Their only enemies are people and wild dogs called dingoes. Kangaroos are protected by law. But when there are a great many kangaroos, some hunting is allowed.

Kangaroos carry their babies in a pouch.

Karate. See Martial arts.

Kansas

• •

Kansas (blue) ranks 14th in size among the states.

State flag

State seal

State bird
Western meadowlark

Kansas is a state in the Midwestern region of the United States. It lies in the center of the country between Colorado and Missouri. Nebraska lies to the north, and Oklahoma lies to the south.

Kansas is called the *Sunflower State* for the yellow prairie flowers that grow there. Kansas is also called the *Wheat State* because it grows more wheat than any other state.

Topeka is the capital of Kansas. The city lies in northeastern Kansas, an area of gently rolling hills. Topeka is an important trade center. The city's factories make farm machinery, pet foods, potato chips, steel

The plains of Kansas produce huge harvests of wheat. Kansas is called the *Wheat State* and the *Breadbasket of America.*

products, and tires. Wichita, the largest city in Kansas, is a major manufacturing center. Many airplanes are made in Wichita. The Arkansas River flows through the middle of the city.

Land. Most of Kansas is a rolling plain, with some low hills. Long ago, huge sheets of ice called glaciers covered Kansas. The glaciers moved very slowly, flattening the land and filling the valleys. The glaciers also made the soil very rich for farming.

Kansas has many rivers and streams. The Kansas River flows through northern Kansas. The Arkansas River flows through the southern part of the state. Huge cottonwood trees line the banks of the streams and rivers.

Resources and products. Kansas grows many kinds of crops in its rich soil. Wheat, the state's leading crop, is grown in every part of Kansas. Farmers also grow corn, grain sorghum, soybeans, hay, and sugar beets. Hay and grain sorghum are used to feed beef cattle and hogs. Kansas is a leading cattle state.

Manufacturing plants in Kansas make airplanes, truck parts, snowplows, and trailers. Also, many plants make food products from the state's crops and livestock. Kansas also produces oil and natural gas.

Facts About Kansas

Capital: Topeka.

Area: 82,282 sq. mi. (213,110 km²).

Population: 2,485,600.

Year of statehood: 1861.

State abbreviations: Kans. or Kan. (traditional), KS (postal).

State motto *Ad Astra per Aspera* (To the Stars Through Difficulties).

State song: "Home on the Range." Words by Brewster Higley; music by Daniel Kelley.

Largest cities: Wichita, Kansas City, Topeka.

Government:

State government:
Governor: 4-year term.
State senators: 40; 4-year terms.
State representatives: 125; 2-year terms.
Counties: 105.

Federal government:
U.S. senators: 2.
U.S. representatives: 4.
Electoral votes: 6.

Important dates in Kansas

Indian days	Before white settlers came, several Indian tribes lived in what is now Kansas. These included the Kansa, Pawnee, and Wichita tribes.
1541	Spanish explorer Francisco Vasquez de Coronado entered Kansas.
1803	The United States purchased the Louisiana Territory, which included what is now Kansas, from France.
1821	William Becknell set up the Santa Fe Trail. Many early settlers crossed the Kansas region along this trail.
1850's	People in the Kansas region fought over whether slavery should be legal in the region. This fighting gave the area the nickname Bleeding Kansas.
1854	Congress established the Territory of Kansas.
1861	Kansas became the 34th state on January 29.
1870's	Immigrants from Russia planted and raised the first Turkey Red wheat in Kansas. This kind of wheat could be farmed easily in the state. Kansas became the leading U.S. producer of wheat.
1894	People began mining oil and natural gas, two major sources of energy, in Kansas. The state became an important mining center.
1934-1935	Dust storms damaged large areas of Kansas farmland.
1990	Joan Finney became the first woman to be elected governor of Kansas.

The first Indian-language newspaper, the *Siwinowe Kesibwi* (Shawnee Sun) was printed in Kansas in 1835.

State flower
Sunflower

Other articles to read: **Coronado, Francisco Vasquez de; Louisiana Purchase.**

Kazakhstan

● ●

Facts About Kazakhstan

Capital: Astana.

Area: 1,049,156 sq. mi. (2,717,300 km²).

Population: Estimated 1998 population— 17,457,000.

Official language: Kazakh.

Climate: Dry, with very cold winters and long, hot summers.

Chief products:

Agriculture: grain, meat, wool.

Manufacturing: chemicals, food products, heavy machinery.

Mining: coal, copper, lead, natural gas, petroleum.

Form of government: Republic.

Flag

Kazakhstan and its neighbors

Kazakhstan (*kah zahk STAHN*) is a country that lies mostly in west-central Asia. It borders the Caspian Sea in the southwest. Russia lies to the west and north. China is to the east. Turkmenistan, Uzbekistan, and Kyrgyzstan lie to the south.

Kazakhstan's land varies greatly from west to east. Dry lowlands cover much of the western and southwestern regions. High, grassy plains called steppes (*STEHPS*) blanket large areas of the north, and sandy deserts cover much of the south. Northeastern Kazakhstan has high, flat lands that are good for farming. Mountain ranges form the nation's eastern and southeastern borders. Astana is the capital, but Almaty is the largest city.

In the cities, most Kazakhs live in modern apartments or houses. In the villages, most people live in houses. But some Kazakh shepherds still live in tentlike houses called yurts, which can be moved from place to place.

Agriculture is a major money-making activity in Kazakhstan. Important industries in Kazakhstan include those that make food and mine minerals. Bauxite, iron, and coal are mined in Kazakhstan. Petroleum and gas are found near the Caspian Sea. People use coal, petroleum, and gas for heating homes, running machines, and other purposes.

For hundreds of years, the Kazakh people worked as herders. They were nomads who wandered across the plains with their sheep, camels, cattle, and horses. They relied on their animals for food, clothing, and transportation. This lifestyle began to change in the 1800's, when Russia conquered the Kazakh region. Kazakhstan became part of the Soviet Union in 1922. While Kazakhstan was under Soviet rule, industry grew steadily. Most of the Kazakh people stopped working as herders and settled in villages or cities. In 1991, Kazakhstan declared its independence from the Soviet Union.

Keller, Helen

Helen Keller (1880-1968) is a great example of a person who overcame disabilities. Although she was blind and deaf, she became a famous author and speaker. Keller worked all her life to help other blind and deaf people.

Helen Keller was born in Tuscumbia, Alabama. As a baby, she developed a serious illness that destroyed her sight and hearing. Because of this, she was completely shut off from things around her. For almost five years, she was a wild child. She could only scream, giggle, kick, and scratch to make her feelings known.

When Helen was about 7 years old, her father hired a teacher named Anne Sullivan. Sullivan made contact with Helen through the sense of touch. The teacher used a sign-language alphabet to spell words into Helen's hand. Slowly, Helen understood that certain hand movements stood for letters, that groups of letters made words, and that words stood for people and things. Once she understood this, Helen made fast progress. Within three years, she could read and write in braille, the form of reading and writing used by blind people. By the time she was 16, she had learned to speak. She went to college and graduated with top grades.

After college, Helen worked to better the lives of blind and deaf people. She appeared before government leaders. She gave speeches and wrote many books and articles. During World War II (1939-1945), she worked with soldiers who had been blinded in battle. Wherever she spoke, she brought new courage to blind and deaf people.

Other articles to read: **Blindness; Braille; Sign language.**

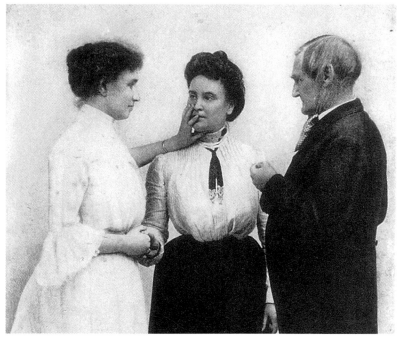

Helen Keller "listened" to speech with her hands. Here, she and her teacher Anne Sullivan show actor Joseph Jefferson her method.

Kennedy, John Fitzgerald

● ●

President John Fitzgerald Kennedy at a press conference in 1963.

John Fitzgerald Kennedy (1917-1963) served as the 35th president of the United States, from 1961 to 1963. He was assassinated, or murdered, after serving less than three years as president.

Kennedy was the youngest man ever elected to be the U.S. president, and he was the youngest to die in that office.

John Kennedy was born in Brookline, Massachusetts. He came from a political family whose ancestors were farmers in Ireland. During World War II (1939-1945), he was the skipper of a U.S. Navy boat in the South Pacific. A Japanese destroyer cut the boat in two, and Kennedy led his crew to safety. He returned home as a war hero. Kennedy was elected to the U.S. House of Representatives in 1946. He served until 1952, when he was elected to the Senate.

Kennedy became president in 1961. He was a strong leader and won great respect throughout the world. In 1962, the United States learned that the Soviet Union had set up nuclear missiles in Cuba. People feared that the Soviet Union might

Kennedy debated Richard M. Nixon on television during the 1960 presidential race.

use these missiles to bomb the United States. But Kennedy demanded that the Soviets take out the missiles, and they were removed.

At home, the United States was very prosperous. African Americans made great progress in their struggle for equal rights. While Kennedy was president, the United States also made its first manned space flights and prepared to send astronauts to the moon.

On November 22, 1963, Kennedy visited Dallas, Texas. As he rode in an open car with his wife, Jackie, three shots rang out. The president was struck in the head and neck and died soon after. The murder of this young, popular president shocked the world.

Kennedy, Robert F.

Robert F. Kennedy (1925-1968) served as attorney general of the United States from 1961 to 1964. As attorney general, he was the chief law officer of the United States. He helped make sure that people obeyed the country's laws. Robert Kennedy also served in the U.S. Senate from 1965 to 1968.

Kennedy was born in Brookline, Massachusetts. Many members of his family held public office. His brother, John F. Kennedy, was president of the United States from 1961 to 1963. Robert— also known as Bobby—acted as his brother's closest personal adviser when John Kennedy was president. Another brother, Edward M. "Ted" Kennedy, has been a member of the U.S. Senate since 1962.

Robert Kennedy was murdered in Los Angeles in June 1968. At the time, he was trying to run for president of the United States.

Robert F. Kennedy campaigned for his brother John F. Kennedy in 1960.

Kentucky

Frankfort

Kentucky (blue) ranks 37th in size among the states.

State flag

State seal

Kentucky is one of the Southern States of the United States. Illinois, Indiana, and Ohio lie to the north. Tennessee borders Kentucky on the south. Virginia and West Virginia lie to the east. Missouri lies to the west.

Kentucky is often called the *Bluegrass State* for the bluish-green grass that grows there. The state also has many horse farms where race horses graze in fields of bluegrass.

Frankfort, the capital of Kentucky, lies in north-central Kentucky, just east of Louisville. Louisville is Kentucky's largest city and an important center for trade and industry. It is also famous for Churchill Downs, where the Kentucky Derby, a famous horse race, is run every year.

Kentucky is also known for two natural wonders— Mammoth Cave and Cumberland Falls.

Kentucky horse farms produce some of the world's finest thoroughbred race horses.

Land. North-central Kentucky has rich farmland and the state's biggest cities. The northwestern region is rich in coal. The state's westernmost region has low hills and some swamps and lakes. Southern Kentucky has flat farmland and some rocky ridges. The Appalachian Mountains rise in the southeast.

Resources and products. Many areas of Kentucky have rich soil, and farming is a leading industry. Tobacco is Kentucky's most important farm product. Farmers also grow corn, wheat and other grains; soybeans; and fruits and vegetables.

Livestock farmers raise beef cattle, chickens, and hogs. Around Lexington, they breed and sell race horses. The grass and water in this area have many minerals that give horses strong bones and muscles.

Kentucky also has many coal fields. These large coal deposits make Kentucky a leading coal producer.

Kentucky factories make many products, such as cars, trucks, and airplane parts. They also make chemicals, machinery, and printed materials.

Important dates in Kentucky

Indian days	Native Americans lived in the Kentucky region for thousands of years before the first Europeans arrived. These peoples included the Cherokee, Delaware, Iroquois, and Shawnee tribes.
1750	American pioneer Thomas Walker explored what is now eastern Kentucky.
1767	American pioneer Daniel Boone made his first journey to Kentucky.
1774	Harrodsburg, Kentucky's first permanent white settlement, was founded.
1775-1783	Frontier leaders defended Kentucky settlements against Indian attacks during the Revolutionary War.
1792	Kentucky became the 15th state on June 1.
1815	The *Enterprise*, the first steamboat to travel up the Mississippi and Ohio rivers, reached Louisville from New Orleans.
1861-1865	Kentucky remained part of the United States during the Civil War.
1936	The U.S. government established a gold vault at Fort Knox.
1955	Kentucky allowed 18-year-olds to vote.
1990	Kentucky began a program to change its public school system. This program included setting up preschool classes for poor families and putting more money into special education programs for children with learning problems.

Facts About Kentucky

Capital: Frankfort.

Area: 40,411 sq. mi. (104,665 km²).

Population: 3,698,969.

Year of statehood: 1792.

State abbreviations: Ky. or Ken. (traditional), KY (postal).

State motto: *United We Stand, Divided We Fall.*

State song: "My Old Kentucky Home." Words and music by Stephen Collins Foster.

Largest cities: Louisville, Lexington, Owensboro.

Government:
State government:
Governor: 4-year term.
State senators: 38; 4-year terms.
State representatives: 100; 2-year terms.
Counties: 120.

Federal government:
U.S. senators: 2.
U.S. representatives: 6.
Electoral votes: 8.

State bird
Kentucky cardinal

State flower
Goldenrod

Abraham Lincoln was born in a cabin in Kentucky in 1809.

In 1775, Daniel Boone led settlers to Kentucky and founded the city of Boonesborough.

Other articles to read: **Appalachian Mountains; Boone, Daniel.**

Kenya

Kenya (*KEHN yuh* or *KEEN yuh*) is a country on the east coast of Africa. It stretches west from the Indian Ocean to Uganda. Tanzania lies to the south, Ethiopia lies to the north, and Somalia lies to the northeast.

Land. Kenya's coastal area is hot and humid. Beautiful sandy beaches, swamps, and patches of rain forest line the coast. Inland, huge grassy plains stretch over most of the land. This area of scattered bushes, shrubs, and grasses is the driest part of Kenya. A highland region of mountains, valleys, and high, flat plains rises in the southwest. Forests and grasslands cover much of this region. The highland has good farmland, and most of Kenya's people live there.

Kenya is famous for its wildlife. Its plains and highlands are home to antelope, buffaloes, cheetahs, elephants, giraffes, leopards, lions, rhinoceroses, and zebras. Crocodiles and hippopotamuses live where there is plenty of water. Many large birds, such as eagles, ostriches, and storks, and dozens of species of small, brightly colored birds also live in Kenya.

People. Almost all Kenya's people are black Africans. They belong to about 40 different ethnic groups. These groups speak different languages and have many different ways of life. Kenyans value large families. Many Kenyan families have six or more children.

Most of Kenya's people live in the rural areas, or the countryside. The rest live in cities and towns. Most of the rural people live on small farm settlements. They raise crops and animals for a living. A small number of people are nomads who move from place to place in search of grazing land and water for their animals. Most city people work in stores, factories, and business or government offices.

Resources and products. Manufacturing is growing in importance in Kenya. At present, more Kenyans work as farmers than in any other type of job. Coffee and tea are

Facts About Kenya

Capital: Nairobi.

Area: 224,081 sq. mi. (580,367 km²).

Population: Estimated 1998 population— 30,738,000.

Official language: English.

Climate: Tropical, with wet and dry areas; mild and wet in the highlands.

Chief products:

Agriculture: bananas, beef, cassava, coffee, corn, pineapples, sisal, sugar cane, tea, wheat.

Manufacturing: cement, chemicals, cloth, light machinery, processed foods, petroleum products.

Form of government: Republic.

Flag

the most important money-making crops. About one-third of the nation's income comes from farming. Service industries, such as banking, government, tourism, and trade, are also important.

Tourism is a major source of money for Kenya. More than 500,000 tourists visit Kenya every year. They come to enjoy its scenic coast and especially to see its amazing wildlife.

History. Scientists have found the bones of some of the earliest known human beings in Kenya. The scientists think that people probably lived there about 2 million years ago.

About 3,000 years ago, people from other parts of Africa began moving into the Kenya area. These groups became the ancestors of today's Kenyans. They included farmers, herders, and hunters.

Traders from Arabia came to Kenya's coast about 2,000 years ago. Arabs took control of the coastal area in the 700's and ruled it for hundreds of years.

The British ruled Kenya from 1895 to 1963. They set up schools in Kenya like the schools in Great Britain, and many Europeans started large farms in Kenya.

In 1963, Kenya became independent, or free from British rule. Since independence, the leaders of Kenya have encouraged people from the country's ethnic groups to join together as Africans.

Other articles to read: **Lake Victoria; Nairobi.**

Most of Kenya's people live in small farm settlements.

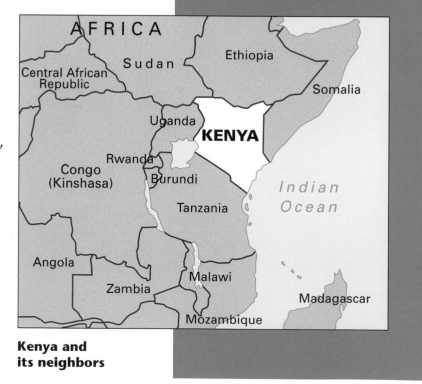

Kenya and its neighbors

Key, Francis Scott

● ●

Francis Scott Key (1779-1843) became famous for writing the words of "The Star-Spangled Banner"—the national anthem, or official song, of the United States.

Francis Scott Key was born in what is now Carroll County, Maryland. While he was working as a lawyer in Washington, D.C., the War of 1812 broke out between the United States and Great Britain. One night, Key watched from a ship while British ships attacked Fort McHenry in Baltimore Harbor, Maryland. He knew that the fort had little defense. The next morning, when he saw that the American flag still flew above the fort, he was overjoyed. Key wrote a poem about the experience. He made it into a song by borrowing a tune from a popular song of the time. In 1931, the U.S. government chose the song as the U.S. national anthem.

The Star-Spangled Banner, the flag in Francis Scott Key's poem, hangs in Washington, D.C. It can be seen at the National Museum of American History, which is part of the Smithsonian Institution. The flag is 50 feet (15 meters) long.

Francis Scott Key

Keyboard instruments

Keyboard instruments make music by means of keys arranged in rows. The keys are usually pieces of wood, plastic, or other material. They are connected with a device that can make sounds. A person plays musical notes by pressing a key.

The most popular keyboard instruments include the piano, harpsichord, and pipe organ. The keys on a piano make small hammers inside the piano move. The hammers make sounds by striking the strings. On a harpsichord, the keys control a small piece of leather or other material that makes sounds by plucking, or pulling, the strings. Pressing a key on a pipe organ opens a pipe through which a column of air vibrates, or moves quickly back and forth, and produces sounds.

Other articles to read: **Piano.**

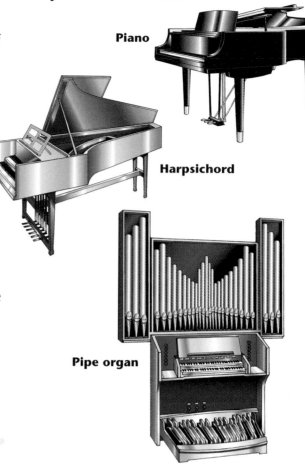

Keyboard Instruments

Piano

Harpsichord

Pipe organ

Kidney

Kidneys are organs, or body parts, in human beings and in all other living things that have backbones. The most important job of the kidneys is the production of urine. Urine is a fluid that carries wastes out of the body. If one kidney is lost in an accident or by disease, the other may grow larger and do the work of both. If both kidneys are damaged or lost, poisons build up in the person's body, leading to death. However, many people with damaged kidneys are kept alive by a dialysis machine. It does the work of the kidneys. Some people get a kidney transplant. Then they have a healthy kidney again.

The kidneys of human beings look like large purplish-brown kidney beans. They are about the size of a grown-up's fist. They lie below the middle of the back on each side of the backbone.

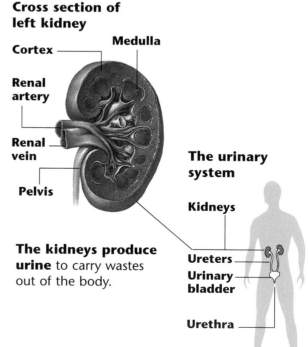

Cross section of left kidney

Cortex

Medulla

Renal artery

Renal vein

Pelvis

The kidneys produce urine to carry wastes out of the body.

The urinary system

Kidneys

Ureters

Urinary bladder

Urethra

Kilimanjaro

Kilimanjaro (*KIHL uh muhn JAHR oh*) is Africa's highest mountain. It is in northern Tanzania, on the Kenya border.

Kilimanjaro has two mountaintops. The higher one, Kibo, rises 19,340 feet (5,895 meters) high at Uhuru Peak. It is always covered by snow and ice, even though it is near the equator. The other mountaintop, Mawensi, has no snow or ice.

Kilimanjaro is a volcano, but it is not active. It has rich soil on its slopes and receives heavy rainfall. Farmers raise bananas and coffee on the lower slopes.

Many people visit the wildlife parks around Kilimanjaro. Ernest Hemingway, an American author, used it in a famous short story, "The Snows of Kilimanjaro."

Kilimanjaro is an inactive volcano.

Killer whale

Killer whales, also called orcas (*AWR kuhz*), are large sea animals. They live in all the oceans, especially in cold waters. They are mammals, animals that feed their young on mother's milk.

Killer whales are up to 30 feet (9 meters) long. They weigh up to 10 tons (9 metric tons). They have shiny black backs, and they are white underneath.

Killer whales have teeth. They feed on salmon, other fish, and sometimes small seals, dolphins, and whales. They have not been known to attack people, however.

Killer whales often travel in groups called pods. Each pod is made up of several females and their young. Every pod has its own "language," or set of underwater sounds.

Killer whale

Kindergarten

Kindergarten is the grade before first grade in school. In kindergarten, children learn by talking, playing, and doing many other things. In many kindergartens, time is set aside every day to talk about interesting things the children have seen and done. They are also given special jobs to do, like helping with snacks. The teacher helps children learn to work together.

Kindergarten children often take trips to learn about things. They may look at plants and animals, go through a supermarket, or visit a post office. They learn numbers by counting, measuring, and comparing things.

Kindergarten teachers talk with parents about how their children are growing and learning. Teachers may visit the children's homes, or parents may visit the school.

Other articles to read: **Nursery school.**

This kindergarten teacher is reading a story to her students.

King

Kings are men who hold titles of great power or honor. A king's wife is called a queen. In many countries, people believed that the king came from a family of gods. In the ancient tribes of Europe, a king was elected by the people during times of war. When these people became Christians, the king's power grew greater. He was thought to speak and act for God. It was his duty to make sure the people followed God's teachings.

Today, some areas are ruled by powerful kings. In other places, such as the United Kingdom and other European countries, kings or queens have little real power. But they do have important positions in their countries.

Other articles to read: **Crown; Queen.**

King Louis XIV of France

King Fahd of Saudi Arabia

King, Martin Luther, Jr.

Martin Luther King, Jr. won the 1964 Nobel Peace Prize for leading peaceful protests.

Martin Luther King, Jr., was a great speaker.

Martin Luther King, Jr. (1929-1968), was an important civil rights leader in the United States. He fought for the freedoms and rights of African Americans and other people. King won the 1964 Nobel Peace Prize for leading peaceful protests. Today, the United States celebrates King's birthday with a national holiday on the third Monday in January.

King was born on January 15, 1929, in Atlanta, Georgia. He became a Baptist minister in 1948. In 1955, King received a Ph.D. degree from Boston University in Massachusetts. At that time, African Americans were treated unfairly in many ways. In some parts of the United States, they were not allowed to use the same schools, hotels, and restaurants as whites. Many people also tried to keep blacks from voting. King worked in peaceful ways to fight against this unfair treatment. He was a great speaker, and he was always against the use of violence as a way to get fair treatment for African Americans. Through the work of King and others, the Civil Rights Act of 1964 and other laws were passed to protect people's rights.

Though King encouraged peaceful action, many people used violence against him. Some people threw rocks at him and bombed his home. On April 4, 1968, King was shot and killed in Memphis, Tennessee. His widow, Coretta Scott King, continues his work of supporting civil rights.

Other articles to read: **Civil Rights; Martin Luther King, Jr., Day.**

King, William Lyon Mackenzie

William Lyon Mackenzie King (1874-1950) was a prime minister of Canada. He headed Canada's government for 21 years, longer than any other prime minister. King was the leader of Canada's Liberal Party.

Mackenzie King was born in Berlin (now Kitchener), Ontario, on December 17, 1874. He received a degree from the University of Toronto, and he also studied in the United States and England. While in college, King developed an interest in the problems of workers and the poor.

As deputy minister of labour in 1900, King helped workers. He helped organize Canada's first Department of Labour. King was elected to Parliament, Canada's lawmaking body, in 1908. He lost his seat in Parliament in 1911, but he continued to work for the Liberal Party.

King became prime minister on Dec. 29, 1921. He served from 1921 to 1926, from 1926 to 1930, and from 1935 to 1948. As prime minister, King helped guide Canada to independence from Britain. Canada became an independent country in 1931. King made important trade agreements with the United States and Britain. He skillfully led Canada through World War II (1939-1945) and helped English-speaking and French-speaking Canadians understand one another better.

King retired as prime minister in November 1948. But he remained a member of Parliament until April 1949. He died on July 22, 1950.

William Lyon Mackenzie King

King Arthur. See Arthur, King.

King Tut. See Tutankhamen.

Kiribati

● ●

Kiribati (*KIHR uh BAS*) is a small country in the middle of the Pacific Ocean. It is made up of 33 islands. Kiribati has three island groups: (1) the Gilbert Islands and Banaba, (2) the Phoenix Islands, and (3) the Line Islands. Most of the country's people live in the Gilbert Islands. Tarawa, an island in the Gilbert Islands, is Kiribati's capital.

Almost all the islands of Kiribati are coral islands. Coral is a stony substance made of the skeletons of tiny sea creatures. The islands are low and flat. Many are ring-shaped.

The language of the islanders is Gilbertese, but most people also speak some English. English is the official language, used in government and business. Most of the people live in small villages. Many homes are made of wood and leaves from coconut trees. Some people have cement-block houses with iron roofs.

Fishing is an important part of life for the people of Kiribati. They also make and sail canoes. The islanders grow most of their own food, which includes bananas, breadfruit, papaya (*puh PY uh*), sweet potatoes, and a plant with a starchy, underground stem called giant taro (*TAH roh*). They also raise pigs and chickens.

People have lived on what is now Kiribati for hundreds of years. Great Britain took control of much of what is now Kiribati in 1892. Kiribati became independent on July 12, 1979.

Facts About Kiribati

Capital: Tarawa.

Area: 280 sq. mi. (726 km²).

Population: Estimated 1998 population—84,000.

Official language: English; Gilbertese is also spoken.

Climate: Hot and wet all year around. Northern islands receive more than twice as much rainfall as the other islands.

Chief products:

Agriculture: bananas, breadfruit, chickens, copra, giant taro, papaya, pandanus fruit, pigs, sweet potatoes.

Mining: phosphate rock.

Form of government: Republic.

Flag

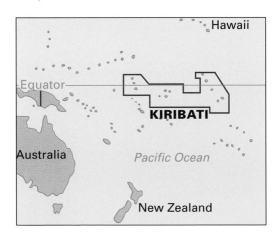

Kiribati and its neighbors

Kite

● ●

A kite is an object that is flown in the air at the end of a string. Kites may be made of paper, cloth, or plastic. Many have a light frame made of wood. The frame may also be plastic, fiberglass, or aluminum. Kites should be flown in open spaces, far from electric lines or antennas. The name *kite* comes from a graceful, soaring bird called a *kite*.

Kites probably were first used in China more than 2,000 years ago. Most people fly kites for fun, but kites are also flown in contests. They have been used in scientific experiments, too.

Kites can be made in hundreds of sizes, shapes, and colors. The flat kite is the oldest and simplest kind. It has a tail that helps keep the kite pointed upward. A simple tail consists of cloth strips tied together and attached to the bottom of the kite. The more wind there is, the longer the tail should be.

To fly a kite, one person holds the kite while another, called the flier, holds the string and walks about 50 steps away. The wind should be blowing at the back of the flier and in the face of the person holding the kite. The flier pulls the string tight, and the kite is released. The kite rises while the flier lets out the string slowly. If the kite begins to fall, the flier should loosen the string. To bring the kite down, the flier walks toward the kite while pulling in the string.

For safety reasons, kites should never be flown in stormy or wet weather.

Framework

Horizontal strut

Bridle

Vertical strut

Covering

Flying Line

Tail

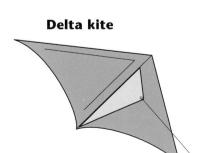

Delta kite

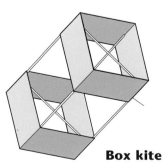

Box kite

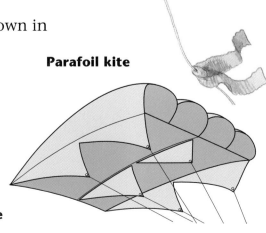

Parafoil kite

Kiwi

A kiwi (*KEE wee*) is a berry with brown, fuzzy skin. Inside, it has bright green pulp, or soft flesh, and tiny black seeds. A kiwi is about the same size and shape as an egg. The fruit has a pleasant flavor, but some are a bit sour. Kiwis are rich in vitamin C, like oranges.

People eat kiwis fresh, frozen, or canned. Kiwis are often used in fruit salads, pies, ice cream, and wine.

Kiwis grow on vines. The plants grow best in places where the weather is not too hot or too cold. New Zealand is the world's biggest producer of kiwi.

Kiwi flowers and fruit

Knight

Knights were male soldiers who fought on horseback. They lived in Europe many years ago. A knight wore a suit of metal called armor to protect him. He rode a huge war horse. Knights fought with swords, shields, and wooden spears called lances.

The best knights were brave, good, well-mannered, and kind. They were faithful to God and their country. They treated women with respect, protected the weak, and were fair to enemies. Some knights did not behave this way, however. Some were very cruel, especially toward people of low rank.

Knights lived during the later part of the Middle Ages. The Middle Ages lasted between the 400's and the 1500's. Between 1100 and 1300, most knights became servants to lords, or people of high rank.

Some men were made knights on the battlefield if they had shown great bravery. But most began

A joust is a fight between two knights.

Training for knighthood

A boy was a page from age 7. A page learned to fight, play skill games like chess, serve his master, and hunt.

As a teenager, a page became a squire. A squire served his master and trained as a knight.

With the words, "I dub you knight," the squire became a knight.

The best knights were brave, good, well-mannered, and kind.

Today, British subjects may be knighted for achievement in the arts, the sciences, sports, and business, as well as for military distinction. Musician Paul McCartney, *above*, received a medal of knighthood in 1997.

training as boys. When a boy reached the age of 7, he left home and lived in the home of a knight or person of high rank. There, he learned the skills and behavior of a good knight.

A knight's job was to fight in times of war. In the early days of knighthood, the knight wore heavy clothing of padded fabric or leather, covered with mail, or chains of metal rings. His helmet had a flap that covered his nose.

Later, armor became heavier and covered more of the body. In the 1400's, metal armor covered the knight's body completely. The suit of armor was so heavy that a knight had to be lifted onto his horse by a crane. If he fell off during battle, he could not get up without help. On his shield and outer clothing, he wore a coat of arms. The coat of arms identified his family. When the face of a knight in battle was completely covered, the coat of arms was the only way to recognize him.

In times of peace, knights passed the time by practicing for war. They took part in tournaments, which were fights between two groups of knights. These fights were like real battles, and they provided valuable training. But kings did not like tournaments, because they were bloody and wasteful. Kings also feared the power of large groups of knights. As a result, tournaments could be held only with permission from the king.

Knights also had jousts (*jowsts*), which were fights between two knights. Many people liked to watch jousts. Tilting also became popular. In tilting, two knights on horseback galloped toward each other in narrow lanes. Each knight tried to knock the other off his horse.

Other articles to read: **Armor; Arthur, King; Coat of arms; Crusades.**

Knitting

• •

Knitting is a way of making fabric by looping yarns around each other. The yarn is linked together by knitting needles. Much of our clothing is knitted, including sweaters, scarves, and hats. Knitted clothes are popular because they are warm and comfortable. They can stretch, too.

People who knit use two long, pointed knitting needles to make a flat piece of fabric. They use three or four needles to knit round, hollow items, such as socks. They may also use needles with a circle shape. Knitters may use slender needles and lightweight yarn for baby clothes. They use thick needles and heavy yarn to make a heavy sweater.

Knitting machines use many needles. They can knit much faster than a person can.

How to make a knit stitch:

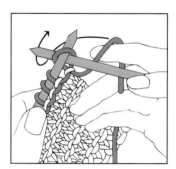

Guide the yarn forward around the tip of the right-hand needle.

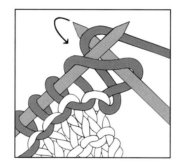

Pull the yarn through the top stitch, using the tip of the right-hand needle.

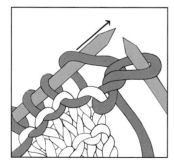

Drop the top stitch off the left-hand needle. Keep the stitch on the other needle.

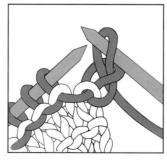

A complete knit stitch is shown above. Repeat these steps for each new stitch.

Pretty Knitting Boxes

You can make pretty boxes to hold yarn for knitting.

Collect some round boxes big enough to hold a ball of yarn. Cover each box and lid with contact paper, which sticks by itself. Or glue a piece of cloth around each box.

Cut a small hole in the center of each lid. Then cut holes on opposite sides of each box, near the top.

Glue ribbon around the edge. Use a different color for each box.

Use more ribbon to make the handle. Put the ends of the ribbon through the holes on the sides. Tie a knot in each end on the inside.

Now put the yarn in the boxes. Match each color of yarn to the color of the ribbon. To use the yarn, pull it through the hole in the lid.

Things You Need:
• round boxes with lids
• contact paper or cloth and glue
• scissors
• ribbon

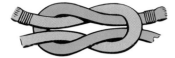

Square knot

Granny knot

Rolling hitch

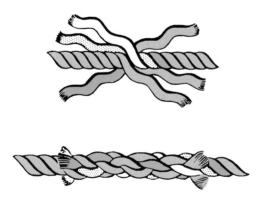

The short splice is the strongest splice. It is used to make a sling by joining two ends of rope.

Knot

A knot is a way to tie ropes, cords, or threads, or to fasten them together. People use knots for many things. Sailors use knots to tie ropes on things that are lifted on or off boats, and to tie the lines attaching their sails. Doctors tie tiny knots in threads used for stitching cuts. Farmers use knots to tie animals to posts. In arts and crafts, people use knots to make clothing, belts and purses, and decorations. People also use knots to tie shoelaces, set up tents, prepare fishing tackle, and to do hundreds of other jobs.

There are many types of knots. The square knot is probably the best known and most widely used knot. It joins the ends of two ropes. People use the square knot because it is strong and it is easy to tie and untie. People use square knots to tie packages and many other things. The square knot is also used in a type of craft called macramé (*MAK ruh may*).

Knots are one of the oldest inventions. Early people used them to tie arrowheads to the arrow shafts, and to tie bowstrings, or cords, to bows. Other early uses of knots included making clothes and fishing nets, and binding wood together to make a shelter.

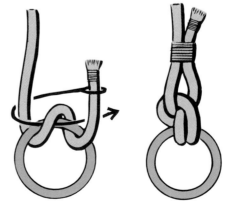

Fisherman's bend is a strong, safe knot used to tie anchors and fishhooks.

Koala

A koala (*koh AH luh*) is a small animal found in Australia. It is sometimes called a bear, but it is not really a bear. Koalas are marsupial (*mahr SOO pee uhl*) mammals. The young koala, called a joey, is carried in a pouch on its mother's belly, and it drinks its mother's milk.

A koala has soft gray or brown fur on its back and white fur on its belly. It has round ears, long toes, and sharp, curved claws. A full-grown koala is 25 to 30 inches (64 to 76 centimeters) tall.

Koalas live in trees and sleep most of the day. They are active at night. Koalas eat the leaves and shoots of eucalyptus (*yoo kuh LIHP tuhs*) trees.

A koala mother carries its baby in its pouch for about seven months. The young koala spends the next six months riding on its mother's back.

Koala

Konigsburg, Elaine

Elaine Konigsburg (*ih LAYN KOH nihgz BURG*) (1930-   ) writes and illustrates children's books. One of her best-known books, *From the Mixed-Up Files of Mrs. Basil E. Frankweiler,* won the 1968 Newbery Medal. It describes the adventures of two children who explore the Metropolitan Museum of Art in New York City. The Newbery Medal is given every year to an American author for an outstanding book for children.

Konigsburg also won the 1997 Newbery Medal for *The View from Saturday,* a book about a group of sixth-graders and their teacher.

Konigsburg was born in New York City. Her other books include *Jennifer, Hecate, Macbeth, William McKinley, and Me, Elizabeth* (1968), *A Proud Taste for Scarlet and Miniver* (1973), and *Throwing Shadows* (1980).

E.L. Konigsburg

Kookaburra

The kookaburra (*KUK uh bur uh*) is the name of a group of birds that live in Australia and New Guinea. Kookaburras are known for their unusual call, which sounds like a loud laugh. The kookaburra is a kind of kingfisher. It is one of Australia's best-known birds.

Kookaburras have large heads, long bills, and brown, black, or white feathers. They are about 17 inches (43 centimeters) long. These birds live in the woods and nest in tree holes. The male birds are fierce, and they defend their homes from enemies.

Kookaburras enjoy a wide variety of foods. They eat caterpillars, fish, frogs, insects, small mammals, snakes, worms, and even small birds.

Kookaburra

Koran. See Quran.

Korbut, Olga

Olga Korbut (1955-   ) is a famous gymnast from the former Soviet Union. She became a star at the 1972 Olympic Games in Munich, Germany. Korbut was known for her daring back flips. She became the first person ever to do a back flip in the gymnastics event called the uneven parallel bars. In this event, gymnasts perform on two bars, one of which is higher than the other.

Korbut was born in Grodno in what is now Belarus. She entered a special school for athletes when she was 11. Korbut won three gold medals and a silver in the 1972 Olympic Games, and a gold and a silver at the 1976 Olympics in Montreal, Canada.

In 1977, Korbut graduated from a teaching school in Grodno. In 1991, she moved to the United States. She coached gymnastics in Atlanta, Georgia.

Olga Korbut performs on the balance beam.

Korea, North

Korea is a land in eastern Asia that is split into two countries—North Korea and South Korea. North Korea's full name is the Democratic People's Republic of Korea. It has a Communist government. In Communist countries, the government owns all or most of the land, factories, and banks. It makes all the rules. Communists believe that everyone is equal under this kind of government.

Land. North Korea lies at the northern end of the Korean Peninsula, a long narrow piece of land that juts into the sea from mainland China. It has seas on two sides—the Sea of Japan to the east, and the Yellow Sea to the west. To the north the country has a long land border with China and a short one with Russia. To the south is the Republic of Korea, usually called South Korea. The land border between the two countries is guarded by troops from both sides.

In the eastern part of North Korea, narrow plains are separated by low hills. The center of the country is a region of mountains and forests. The highest mountain is Paektu Mountain, 9,003 feet (2,744 meters) high. North Korea's longest river, the Yalu, flows westward from this mountain into the Yellow Sea. Most of North Korea's farms and industries are found on the plains and rolling hills of the western region. The capital city, Pyongyang, is also located there.

North Korea and its neighbors

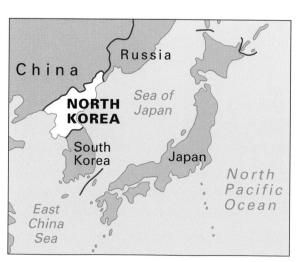

Facts About North Korea

Capital: Pyongyang.

Area: 46,540 sq. mi. (120,538 km²).

Population: Estimated 1998 population—25,121,000.

Official language: Korean.

Climate: Hot and wet in summer, cold and dry in winter.

Chief products:

Agriculture: barley, corn, millet, potatoes, rice, wheat.

Manufacturing: cement, chemicals, cloth, iron and steel, machinery, metals, processed foods.

Mining: coal, iron ore, magnesium, phosphates, salt, tungsten.

Fishing: pollock, sardines, shellfish, squid.

Form of government: Communist.

Flag

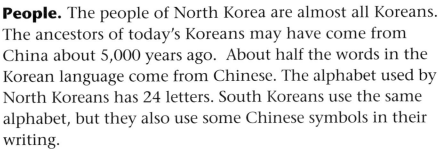

People. The people of North Korea are almost all Koreans. The ancestors of today's Koreans may have come from China about 5,000 years ago. About half the words in the Korean language come from Chinese. The alphabet used by North Koreans has 24 letters. South Koreans use the same alphabet, but they also use some Chinese symbols in their writing.

Most city dwellers in North Korea work in factories. Families usually live in small apartments. Few people live in houses or own cars. Many farmers live on collective farms. These farmers share the work and the crops. There are also some state farms, run by the government.

Most Koreans eat rice for their main meal. They may add fish or vegetables such as beans, but they do not eat meat often. A popular dish is kimchi, a spicy mixture of Chinese cabbage, white radishes, and other vegetables.

The government in North Korea discourages religion. It also forbids any writing or art that does not agree with Communist ideas. Schoolchildren must work for the state during part of their summer vacation.

Resources and products. North Korea mines coal to power the stations that produce much of its electricity. The rest of its energy comes from water power.

Rice is the chief farm crop. Other major crops include barley, corn, potatoes, and wheat. Fishing is important, too.

North Korean factories produce cement, chemicals, cloth, iron and steel, machinery, metals, and processed foods. Most of the country's trade is with China, Japan, and Russia. The government controls nearly all the factories. It also runs the nation's transportation systems, schools, colleges, hospitals, and welfare organizations.

History. Korea was divided into North Korea and South Korea in 1948. [The early history of North Korea and South Korea and the reasons for their division are described in the History section of the article **Korea, South.**] Kim Il Sung became leader of Communist North Korea in 1948.

The Communists took over farms and factories, radio, television, and newspapers. They developed industries and built up large military forces. In 1950, North Korean

This statue of president Kim Il Sung stands in Pyongyang, North Korea's capital city.

troops invaded South Korea. This was the start of the Korean War, which ended in 1953.

The war was followed by many years of suspicion, spying, and outbreaks of fighting between North Korea and South Korea. Plans to make Korea one country again made little progress. In 1991, North and South Korea agreed not to use military force against one another.

Kim Il Sung ruled North Korea as a dictator from 1948 until he died in 1994. He was looked up to as a leader who could do no wrong. After Kim died, his son Kim Jong Il became the national leader.

North Korea has very little contact with other countries. Its people have stayed poor under Communist rule.

Korea, South

• •

Facts About South Korea

Capital: Seoul.

Area: 38,330 sq. mi. (99,274 km²).

Population: Estimated 1998 population—46,262,000.

Official language: Korean.

Climate: Hot and wet in summer, cold and dry in winter. Seasonal winds called monsoons affect weather throughout the year. The east coast is less cold in winter.

Chief products:

Agriculture: apples, barley, Chinese cabbage, melons, onions, potatoes, rice, soybeans, sweet potatoes.

Manufacturing: automobiles, chemicals, cloth and clothing, computer equipment, electrical goods, food products, iron and steel, machinery, plywood, rubber tires, ships, shoes, television sets.

Mining: coal.

Fishing: filefish, oysters, pollock.

Form of government: Republic.

Flag

Korea is a land in eastern Asia that is split into two countries—North Korea and South Korea. South Korea's full name is the Republic of Korea. It is slightly smaller than North Korea, but it has more people.

The plains of South Korea's coastal areas are good farmland.

Land. South Korea lies at the southern end of the Korean Peninsula. North Korea covers the northern part of the peninsula. To the east is the Sea of Japan, and to the west is the Yellow Sea. To the south, the Korea Strait separates South Korea from Japan. South Korea includes many islands. The largest is Cheju Island, in the south. Halla Mountain, South Korea's highest mountain, rises 6,398 feet (1,950 meters) on this island.

Most South Koreans live along the western and southern coasts. These are good farming regions of flat plains and rolling hills. In the center of South Korea are mountains and forests. The capital and largest city is Seoul, with more than 10 million people. Next largest is the industrial city of Pusan, with almost 4 million people.

People. The people of South Korea are almost all Koreans. Some still live in small villages. A country house is usually made of brick or concrete blocks, with heating under the floor. More and more people have moved from the countryside to the cities. Many city people live in high-rise apartments. Others live in suburbs, or towns surrounding the city.

Rice is the main food of most Koreans. People also eat such foods as barley, fish, vegetables, and fruits. Tea is a traditional drink, but many people also drink coffee.

Confucianism, an ancient Chinese way of life and thinking, has many followers in South Korea. It stresses the duties that people have toward one another. About one-fifth of the people are Buddhists, and one-fifth are Christians.

Resources and products. South Korea's most important mineral is anthracite (*AN thruh syt*), a kind of hard coal. The nation gets most of its electricity from power stations that burn coal, gas, and oil. It also has some power stations run by nuclear or water power. The country has a good railroad and road system.

Most farms are small. Many farmers make extra money from fishing. South Korea is a leading fishing nation.

South Korea is one of Asia's fastest-growing industrial countries. Almost all businesses are privately owned. Factories produce many kinds of goods that are sold all over the world. South Korean businesses also run factories in other countries.

History. People lived in Korea at least 30,000 years ago. By about 4,000 years ago, there was a Korean state called Choson. Other kingdoms rose and fell, sometimes coming under Chinese rule.

In the 600's, the southern kingdom of Silla came to control all Korea. It broke apart in the 800's, but in the early 900's, a leader named Wang Kon joined the region together again. He gave Silla a new name—Koryo. The word *Korea* comes from *Koryo*.

South Korea and its neighbors

The giant statue and five-story pagoda at the Popchusa Temple in South Korea's Songnisan National Park.

In 1392, General Yi became king of Koryo. He renamed the country Choson, a name still used by North Koreans. South Koreans call their country Taehan. The dynasty, or line of rulers, founded by Yi lasted until 1910. Then Japan took control of Korea.

Japanese rule lasted until Japan's defeat at the end of World War II (1939-1945). United States soldiers moved into southern Korea. Soviet Union forces took over the north. In 1948, Korea was divided into North Korea and South Korea.

In 1950, North Korea sent its soldiers to attack South Korea, starting the Korean War. The United States and other United Nations forces helped South Korea. China and the Soviet Union helped North Korea. The Korean War ended in 1953.

South Korea developed modern industries. It grew richer than North Korea, but its people had limited freedom. Presidents held wide powers, especially Park Chung Hee (from 1961 to 1979) and Chun Doo Hwan (from 1980 to 1987).

After Chun, more democracy was allowed. In 1988, the Summer Olympic Games were held in South Korea. In the 1990's, South Koreans enjoyed more say in government. But their country struggled to stay successful as a trading nation. Hopes of making the two Koreas one country again remained, in spite of slow progress.

Other articles to read: **Seoul.**

Traditional Korean music features stringed instruments, drums, flutes, and gongs.

Kuwait

Kuwait (*koo WYT* or *koo WAYT*) is a small country at the north end of the Persian Gulf, an inlet of the Indian Ocean. Its neighbors are Iraq and Saudi Arabia. The capital is the city of Kuwait.

Kuwait is mostly waterless desert, but there is water underground. Drinking water is made from seawater by a process called distillation (*dihs tuh LAY shuhn*).

Most of the Kuwaiti people are Arabs. Their religion is Islam. Groups of Palestinians, Egyptians, Asian Indians, and Iranians also live in Kuwait.

Beneath Kuwait's desert is one-tenth of the world's oil. People use oil for heating homes, running machines, and other purposes. Its oil has made Kuwait one of the world's richest nations. Kuwait's people enjoy free education, receive free health and social services, and pay no income tax.

Kuwait's second most important product is natural gas. Natural gas is also used as fuel to heat buildings and run machines. The government has started new industries. There are plans to turn the desert into farmland for crops.

Hardly any people lived in Kuwait before the 1700's, when the British set up a mail service there. Britain took responsibility for Kuwait's defense from 1899 to 1961. After drilling for oil began in 1936, Kuwait changed rapidly from a poor land to a wealthy one. In 1961, Kuwait became independent, or free from British rule.

In August 1990, Iraq invaded Kuwait and tried to make it part of Iraq. This attack led to the Persian Gulf War. Allied forces freed Kuwait in February 1991.

Facts About Kuwait

Capital: Kuwait.

Area: 6,880 sq. mi. (17,818 km²).

Population: Estimated 1998 population—1,702,000.

Official language: Arabic.

Climate: Very hot from April to September, often above 120 °F (49 °C). Coolest in January, averaging between 50 and 60 °F (10 and 16 °C). A little rain falls from October to March.

Chief products: Petroleum and natural gas.

Form of government: Emirate. The government is led by an emir, who is chosen by the members of the ruling family from among themselves.

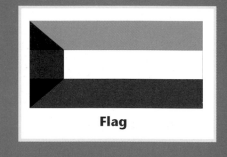

Flag

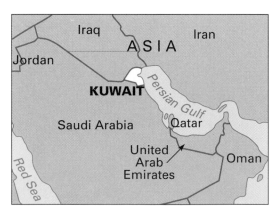

Kuwait and its neighbors

An African-American boy lights his family's Kwanzaa candles.

Kwanzaa

Kwanzaa (*KWAHN zuh*) is an African-American holiday. It is based on an African harvest festival. Kwanzaa begins on December 26 and lasts for seven days.

The idea for the holiday came in 1966 from Professor Maulana Karenga, a teacher of African studies. He listed seven principles, or important ideas, of black culture. They are *Umoja*, meaning unity; *Kujichagulia*, meaning self-determination; *Ujima*, meaning collective work and responsibility; *Ujamaa*, meaning cooperative economics; *Nia*, meaning purpose; *Kuumba*, meaning creativity; and *Imani*, meaning faith.

On each day of Kwanzaa, people think about one of the seven principles. At a feast called *karamu*, people eat typical African food and honor their ancestors. They think back on the old year and enjoy music, songs, and dancing.

Kyoto

Kyoto (*kee OH toh*) is one of Japan's largest cities. It stands on Honshu Island, the largest of the four main islands of Japan.

Kyoto was the capital of Japan from 794 to 1868. The word *Kyoto* is Japanese for *capital city*. The city has many fine, old palaces and religious buildings. One of the most beautiful sights is the Golden Pavilion, built in 1397 as part of a palace and rebuilt in the 1950's. Nijo Castle was built in the 1600's. The Imperial Palace was built for the emperor in 794 and rebuilt in 1855.

Kyoto has many colleges. Its small factories make fine pottery and silk cloth.

The Golden Pavilion in Kyoto, Japan

Kyrgyzstan

Kyrgyzstan (*kihr GEEZ stan*) is a country in central Asia. It lies in the high Tian Shan and Alay mountains. Peak Pobedy, the highest mountain, rises 24,406 feet (7,439 meters), close to the border with China. Bishkek is the capital city and main industrial center.

Most of the country's people live in the lower plains and mountain valleys. Summers are warm and dry there, and winters are less cold than in the mountains. In the north is a large lake called Issyk-Kul.

About half the people of Kyrgyzstan are Kyrgyz. The others are Russians, Uzbeks, Ukrainians, and Germans. The Kyrgyz and Uzbeks are Muslims. Most of the other people are Christians.

The Kyrgyz are farmers and herders. Some live in villages, and others are nomads who wander from place to place for at least part of the year. The nomads carry their tentlike homes, called yurts, with them. They herd sheep, cattle, and goats.

Kyrgyzstan's factories make food products, machinery, and cloth. Its mining products include coal, lead, and oil. There is one railroad, but most people travel by bus.

Beginning in the 1200's, Kyrgyzstan was ruled for hundreds of years by central Asian peoples called the Mongols. During the 1800's, the region became part of the Russian Empire. Kyrgyzstan was part of the Soviet Union from 1922 until 1991. In 1991, Kyrgyzstan became an independent country.

Facts About Kyrgyzstan

Capital: Bishkek.

Area: 76,641 sq. mi. (198,500 km²).

Population: Estimated 1998 population—4,960,000.

Official language: Kyrgyz.

Climate: Warm, dry summers in lowlands, cool in winter. Very cold winters in the mountains.

Chief products:

Agriculture: cattle, cotton, eggs, fruit, goats, grain, milk, sheep, vegetables, wool.

Manufacturing: cloth, construction materials, food products, machinery, metals.

Mining: antimony, coal, mercury, oil.

Form of government: Republic.

Kyrgyzstan and its neighbors

Flag

L

is the twelfth letter of the English alphabet.

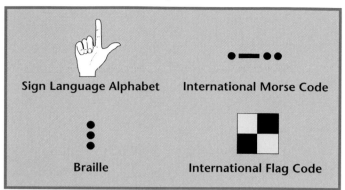

Sign Language Alphabet

International Morse Code

Braille

International Flag Code

Development of the letter L

THE ANCIENT EGYPTIANS	THE SEMITES	THE PHOENICIANS	THE GREEKS	THE ROMANS
about 3000 B.C., drew this symbol of a crooked staff called a *goad*.	about 1500 B.C., changed the Egyptian symbol. They called the letter *lamed,* their word for *goad*.	about 1000 B.C., drew a symbol of an upside-down staff.	changed the Phoenician symbol and added it to their alphabet about 600 B.C. They called the letter *lambda*.	gave the letter L its present form about A.D. 114.

Lace

Lace

Lace is a lovely, netlike fabric made from threads. Today, most lace is made by machines, but some lace is still handmade.

There are two main kinds of handmade lace. One kind is called needlepoint lace, and the other is called bobbin lace.

To make needlepoint lace, a drawing of the design is sewn onto a piece of linen. Then the lacemaker fills in the design with a needle and thread.

To make bobbin lace, the drawing is sewn onto a pillow. Then pins are stuck into the lines of the design. The lacemaker works threads from bobbins, or spools, around the pins to make the lace.

Lacemaking began in Europe about 500 years ago. Many kinds of lace are named for the place where they were first made. For example, a well-known needlepoint lace called Venetian lace was first made in Venice, Italy. A well-known bobbin lace called Chantilly was first made in Chantilly, France.

Lacrosse

● ●

Lacrosse (*luh KRAWS*) is a fast team sport. It is played on a field with goals at either end. Each player carries a stick called a crosse, which has a net pocket at the end. Players use the pocket to catch and throw the ball down the field. Each player may pass, catch, or run with the ball in the pocket. Players on the opposing team may try to gain the ball by knocking it out of the pocket with their own sticks. Only the goalkeeper may touch the ball with the hands. A team scores by putting the ball into the opponent's goal.

A game like lacrosse was played by American Indians hundreds of years ago. In 1867, the modern rules for the game were set by a Canadian lacrosse player named George Beers. The game is popular in colleges and high schools in the United States, where men's collegiate lacrosse began in 1877. The first U.S. women's lacrosse team was formed in 1926.

Lacrosse rules are not the same in every country where the game is played. In U.S. men's lacrosse, there are 10 players on a team. Men may body check, or bump, an opponent, and players wear gloves, helmets, and face masks for protection. A women's team has 12 players. In women's lacrosse, no body contact is allowed.

Lacrosse is a fast-paced field game.

Ladybugs eat harmful insects.

Ladybug

Ladybugs are small insects. They are a kind of beetle. They are also known as ladybirds or lady beetles. They have a round body shaped like half of a pea.

Ladybugs have stiff, leathery wings that are often bright red or yellow. The wings have black, red, white, or yellow spots. These tiny beetles feed mainly on harmful insects. People use ladybugs to get rid of insects that feed on plants.

In the late 1800's, an insect called cottony cushion scale almost destroyed the fruit crops in California. Growers brought ladybugs in to control the harmful insects and save the crops.

Two kinds of ladybugs harm beans, melons, squashes, and other garden plants. But there are many helpful kinds, and ladybugs do much more good than harm.

Lafayette, Marquis de

The Marquis de Lafayette (*mahr KEE deh LAH fih EHT*) (1757-1834) was a French soldier and leader. He helped the Americans in the Revolutionary War (1775-1783), when the thirteen colonies fought for their freedom from British rule.

Lafayette was born in Chavaniac, France, on September 6, 1757. His name was Marie Joseph Paul Yves Roch Gilbert du Motier. His parents and grandfather died when he was young. He received a great fortune from his family and studied at a military academy.

Lafayette did not enjoy the life of a rich man in France. He wanted to win fame by fighting against Great Britain. He bought a ship and sailed to America in 1777 with a group of French soldiers.

Marquis de Lafayette

Lafayette served with General George Washington through the long winter at Valley Forge, Pennsylvania. He led soldiers in several battles. He went back to France in 1779 but returned in 1780. The next year, his troops helped defeat British troops and force Britain's General Cornwallis to give up.

Lafayette returned to France. In 1789, the French Revolution broke out. The people rebelled against their government. Lafayette was in charge of the troops sent to keep order, so he was unpopular with the French people. The king and queen did not trust him, either. In 1792, he left France. When he returned in 1800, he found out that his fortune had been taken by the French government.

Lafayette later was elected to the government by the French voters. He worked to help the American government, and he worked for the independence of many other countries, including Greece, Poland, and South American nations.

Lake

● ●

A lake is a body of water with land all around it. Lakes are found in all parts of the world. Some large bodies of water that are called seas are really lakes. These include the Salton Sea in California and the Sea of Galilee in Israel.

How do lakes come to be? Some lakes were made by glaciers (*GLAY shuhrz*). These slowly moving rivers of ice cut deep valleys into the land. When the ice melts, the valleys fill up with water, becoming lakes. Glaciers made the Great Lakes thousands of years ago.

Upper Ice Lake in the Cascade Mountains of Washington state.

Crater Lake and Wizard Island in Oregon

Sinkholes can also make a lake. Under the ground, a soft rock called limestone can slowly melt away with the rain. When it does, the ground can fall in and make a hole. As water from a stream or river fills the hole, it becomes a lake. Some lakes in Florida were made this way.

Lakes can form in other ways, too. For example, rain water can collect in the craters, or hollows, of dead volcanoes. This is how Crater Lake in Oregon was formed.

A lake creates a wonderful world of its own where animals and plants live and grow. Some lake plants float freely, but some are rooted to the bottom of the lake. Snails, bugs, and fish feed on the plants. Ducks, geese, swans, and other birds swim on the lake. Deer and bears come to the edge of the lake to drink water.

A large lake can affect the climate of land nearby. It can make the climate milder. Then it is not so cold in winter, and not so hot in summer.

Lakes are important for trade and travel, too. American Indians and early European explorers used canoes to explore North America's Great Lakes. Today, tugboats, barges, and ships carry coal, iron, and corn on these lakes.

People use lake water to drink and to water crops. Lakes also give people pleasure. People go to lakes all year to enjoy fishing, swimming, boating, and ice skating.

Other articles to read: **Great Lakes; Lake Victoria; Ocean; River.**

Lake Victoria

Lake Victoria is the biggest lake in Africa. It is also the second largest freshwater lake in the world. Only Lake Superior, in the United States, is larger.

Lake Victoria lies partly in Kenya, partly in Tanzania, and partly in Uganda. The equator crosses the lake. The equator is an imaginary line around the middle of the earth. The lake is the main source, or the starting point, of the Nile River. At its deepest point, Lake Victoria is about 270 feet (82 meters) deep. More than 200 kinds of fish live in its waters.

In 1858, John Hanning Speke, an English explorer, became the first European to reach the lake. He named it after Queen Victoria of Britain.

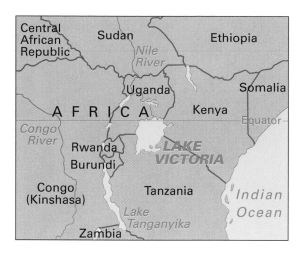

Lake Victoria is the largest lake in Africa.

Lamp

Lamps are things people use to make light. People have used lamps for thousands of years. With lamps, people can work, read, or do other activities after the sun goes down.

Long ago, lamps burned oil or fat. A wick, or cord, made of fibers soaked up the oil or fat. When the wick was lit, it burned and gave off light.

Gas lamps were used in the 1800's. The gas was piped into the lamp. It burned as it rushed out of a small opening and mixed with the air. Today, gas lamps are often used by campers. Such lamps provide light in places that have no electricity.

Thomas Alva Edison, an American inventor, made the first workable electric lamp in the late 1800's. Electric lamps give more light than earlier lamps. They also cost less and are easier to use.

Other articles to read: **Electricity.**

Kerosene lamp

Language

A language laboratory helps students learn to speak and understand a foreign language. Students use tape recorders to record their own voices. They use headphones to listen to their pronunciation or to the pronunciation of the teacher.

Language allows people to talk to each other. It also allows people to write their thoughts and ideas. Wherever there are people, there is language. People who cannot hear or speak may use sign language. They use their hands to make words.

About 6,000 languages are spoken in the world today. English is the language spoken by the greatest number of people. Mandarin Chinese is spoken by many people, too.

How children learn language

Children learn language by hearing and repeating sounds. Babies like to make all kinds of sounds. They hear the people around them speak. They imitate the sounds they hear from the people around them and begin to say words. When they are a little older, they learn that these words have meanings. For example, when a child sees a dog, the child will say the word "dog."

The parts of language

We talk about three things when we talk about language—sounds, words, and structure. Most languages have about 20 to 60 sounds. All languages have words. Words stand for objects, actions, or ideas. Languages also have structure, such as word order. Words come in a certain order: first, second, third, and so on. For example, in English we can say, "The lion roared." First,

Children learn language by hearing and repeating sounds.

we must say "the"; then "lion"; and finally "roared." We cannot change the words around. In some other languages, word order is different.

Writing is a part of some languages, but not of all languages. No language began with writing. Writing always comes after speaking.

The beginning of language

Nobody really knows how language began. It is a mystery. Language probably began very slowly and very early in human history. First, people might have made sounds such as barks, grunts, and hoots. In time, the sounds might have become more exact. Then the sounds came to mean certain things. However, there is no record of early spoken languages. We can only guess about how language began.

We know more about early writing. People have found examples of writing that are over 5,000 years old. Early writing came from Egypt, China, and Sumeria. The earliest writing was in word-pictures.

Many children learn to speak more than one language when their family moves to another country. Children who move to English-speaking countries may attend ESL (English as a Second Language) classes.

Language families

Languages are grouped into families. For example, German and English have many words that are similar. They are both Germanic languages. Long ago, they came from the same parent language, which changed over time.

Italian, French, and Spanish all come from the same parent language. They belong to the Romance group. Hebrew and Arabic belong to the Afro-Asian family.

Other articles to read: **Alphabet; Communication; Dictionary; English language; Hieroglyphics; Punctuation; Sign language; Writing.**

Laos

Facts About Laos

Capital: Vientiane.

Area: 91,429 sq. mi. (236,800 km²).

Population: Estimated 1998 population—5,296,000.

Official language: Lao.

Climate: Hot and wet, with a rainy season from November to March.

Chief products:

Agriculture: cardamom, cattle, citrus fruits, coffee, corn, cotton, rice, tea, tobacco.

Forestry: benzoin, cinchona, teak.

Manufacturing: leather goods, opium, pottery, silk, silver work.

Mining: tin.

Form of government: Republic.

Flag

Laos (*LAH ohs*) is a country in Southeast Asia. It is a tropical land of mountains and thick forests. Laos is bordered by China on the north, Vietnam on the east, Cambodia on the south, and Thailand and Myanmar on the west. Vientiane (*vyehn TYAHN*) is the capital and the largest city.

Some of the people of Laos speak languages similar to Chinese. They include the Lao, Hmong, and Tai people. Other people speak languages similar to those spoken by other people in Southeast Asia and parts of India. They include the Kha people.

About half the people of Laos are Lao. The Lao people are leaders in business and government. The Kha were the first people to live in Laos. Until recently, they were treated badly and had few rights.

Most of the people live in villages and farm for a living. Many farms are on the lowlands along the Mekong River and other rivers. Farmers there raise mainly rice. Most villagers are poor, and some villages have no schools.

Most of the nation's resources have not been developed, and the country has few factories. Old-fashioned methods hold back its farm production.

Ancestors of the Lao and Tai people probably moved into Laos about 1,200 years ago. About 600 years ago, most of what is now Laos was joined together in a kingdom called Lan Xang, which means "land of a million elephants." France took control of Laos during the late 1800's. In 1954, Laos became an independent country.

Laos and its neighbors

La Salle, Sieur de

● ●

Sieur de La Salle (*syur deh luh SAL*) (1643-1687) was a French explorer. He was the first European to follow the Mississippi River to the Gulf of Mexico.

La Salle was born in Rouen, France. His real name was René-Robert Cavelier, but he was known by the name of his family's property. La Salle studied to be a priest. However, he left in 1665 to seek adventure.

La Salle sailed to French Canada and became a wealthy fur trader. American Indians told him of two great rivers, the Mississippi and the Ohio. LaSalle thought one of the rivers might lead to the Pacific Ocean. After he explored the Ohio River, he became sure that the Mississippi River flowed into the Gulf of Mexico instead.

The king of France gave La Salle permission to explore the Mississippi. In 1681, La Salle led a group of explorers down the Illinois River and the Mississippi. They reached the Gulf of Mexico on April 9, 1682. La Salle claimed all the land drained by the Mississippi—and the rivers that ran into it—for France.

In 1684, La Salle sailed from France to start a colony at the point where the Mississippi River flows into the Gulf of Mexico. But he sailed past it, and the settlers landed much farther west. They were attacked by American Indians, and many colonists died from disease. La Salle led a group of people to seek help. Some of the men rebelled against him and killed him.

Sieur de La Salle

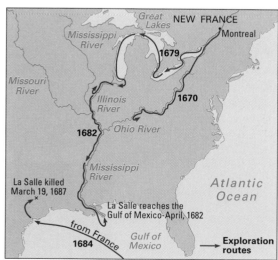

This map shows the explorations of Sieur de La Salle.

Lasers were fired off the Empire State Building in New York on the building's 50th anniversary.

Lasers create an image in a light show.

Laser

A laser is something that makes strong, narrow beams of light. A laser beam is powerful enough to burn a hole in a diamond. A laser beam is narrow enough to drill 200 holes on a pinhead.

The direction of lasers

Most light travels in many directions. For example, light from a light bulb travels in all directions. It shines on all parts of a room. Light from the sun also travels in all directions. When the sun shines, its light covers one half of the earth's surface. Light from a laser is a different kind of light. Laser light travels in only one direction. It travels in a narrow beam like an arrow of light.

The frequency of lasers

Light travels in waves that cannot be seen with the eye alone. Most light travels in waves that move at many different speeds. These wave movements are vibrations—they move quickly back and forth. Most light waves vibrate at different times per second, or at different frequencies. In other words, most light has many frequencies. But the light from a laser usually has only one frequency. Its waves usually move the same number of times per second.

Atoms and lasers

To understand lasers, you have to know something about atoms. Everything in the world is made from atoms. They are like building blocks. Atoms are extremely small. You cannot see them with the eye alone. Atoms store energy, including light. Sometimes atoms give off energy in the form of light, for example. Sometimes they give off this light in such a way that the light goes in only one direction. This is the kind of light a laser makes.

Parts of a laser

To make a laser work, you need power. The power causes atoms to become excited, or move quickly, and give off light. You also need a certain material and a container for the material. The material must have atoms that will easily get excited and give off light in one direction. Crystals or glass are usually used.

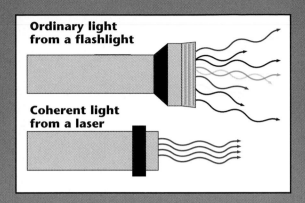

Lasers produce "coherent" light waves. Coherent light waves move in step together and spread only a little.

How does a laser work?

In one type of laser, a powerful flash tube is coiled around a crystal, such as a ruby crystal.

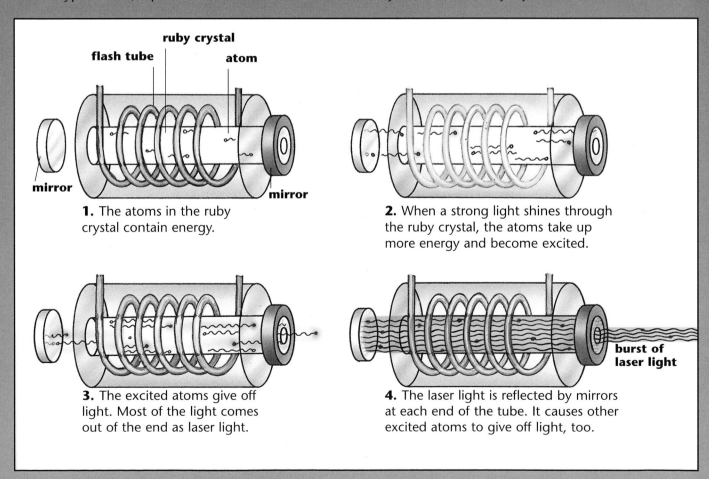

1. The atoms in the ruby crystal contain energy.

2. When a strong light shines through the ruby crystal, the atoms take up more energy and become excited.

3. The excited atoms give off light. Most of the light comes out of the end as laser light.

4. The laser light is reflected by mirrors at each end of the tube. It causes other excited atoms to give off light, too.

Lasers to send messages

A laser can be used to send voice messages and television signals. Its frequency allows it to carry many television programs or telephone voices at the same time. Because its light goes in only one direction, it avoids unwanted noise or interference. Laser light is also used to play compact discs (CD's) and videodiscs.

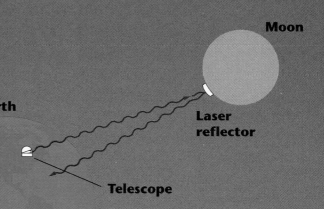

Moon

Earth

Laser reflector

Telescope

Lasers for industry

Lasers are used in industry, too. They can cut tools, such as the teeth in saws. They can drill eyes in needles. They can even guide ships and airplanes with their light. Lasers also create great heat. This heat can be used to melt hard rocks and metals. Welders use laser torches to cut metal and then weld, or melt, it together in a new form.

The distance to the moon can be measured precisely using a laser beam bounced from the earth to a reflector on the moon and back to earth.

Lasers in medicine

A laser beam can burn away sick or dead parts from the body. A laser can also seal up veins so they will not bleed when a doctor does an operation. Eye doctors can fix eye problems with laser beams.

Lasers during war

Lasers are also used by military forces. Soldiers can measure distances and make maps by bouncing light from a laser. They can also bounce laser light off an enemy target to find out how far away it is. Pilots can bounce laser light off an enemy airplane to find out how far away it is and to measure its speed.

This laser reflector was placed on the moon by astronauts.

Lasers in stores

A type of laser is used in supermarket and department stores every day. Laser scanners read the bar codes that tell the price of the items we buy. The scanner also records the items sold by the store. It helps the store clerks keep track of what they need to reorder.

Lasers for art

Lasers can gently clean old works of art that might be harmed by ordinary cleaning. Lasers are also used in holography, a type of photography. The images from holography have three dimensions—they are high, wide, and deep. You may see these images on fancy belt buckles or on advertising posters. You may also see them on credit cards.

Lasers to solve mysteries

Police officers who work in crime labs use lasers to help them solve crimes. They shine laser beams on guns and other objects to look for fingerprints. If the laser beam shows fingerprints, the lab worker photographs them. The fingerprints might help find a criminal or solve a mystery.

The history of lasers

The famous scientist Albert Einstein was the first person to describe the laser. Scientists began to use the idea in the 1950's. The first laser used a ruby rod as the source of power. It was built in 1960. In 1969, space scientists put a special kind of mirror on the moon. They wanted to see if a laser could measure the distance between the earth and the moon. They sent a laser beam from the earth to the moon. The mirror on the moon sent the beam back. Scientists on earth measured the time it took the beam to travel to the moon and come back. That allowed them to figure out the distance from the earth to the moon more exactly. Scientists keep finding new ways to use lasers.

Other articles to read: **Bar coding; Compact disc; Holography.**

A laser scanner reads a bar code at a supermarket.

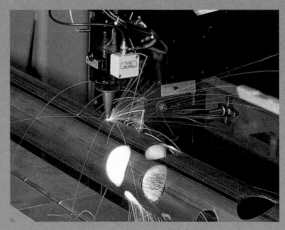

A powerful laser cuts through steel tubing.

Latin America

Latin America

● ●

Latin America is a large region, but it is not a continent. Latin America includes Mexico, Central America, South America, and the islands of the West Indies. Brazil is the largest country in Latin America. Mexico City, Mexico, is Latin America's largest city. Mexico City is also one of the largest cities in the world. Today, most of the people of Latin America speak Spanish or Portuguese. These languages are European, and they came from the Latin language used in ancient Rome. So, because of its languages, this part of the world is called Latin America.

Before 1492, however, Latin languages were not spoken in Latin America. American Indians in this part of the world spoke their own languages. Indians in Latin America included the Aztec, the Maya, and the Inca. Some of these American Indians created art, studied the stars, built roads, and invented ways to write.

Shortly after the first Europeans arrived in Latin America, they brought African slaves to work the land. So today, Latin America has a mixture of customs and people—Africans, American Indians, Europeans, and people whose families are a mixture of these three.

For hundreds of years, Latin American countries were ruled by European countries, especially Spain and Portugal. In the 1800's, many countries fought for freedom and won. Most were not democracies at first. The people had few rights. For example, they did not vote for their leaders. Today, many Latin American countries are democracies.

Other articles to read: **Central America; Mexico City; South America;** and those on the individual countries of Latin America.

The Temple of the Giant Jaguar is among the ruins of Tikal, a great Maya city in Guatemala.

Latitude. See Longitude and latitude.

Latvia

Latvia (*LAT vee uh*) is a country that lies in northern Europe along the Baltic Sea. Estonia and Lithuania border Latvia. Together, these three countries are called the Baltic States. In the east, Latvia also borders Russia and Belarus.

A large plain with many low hills and valleys covers most of Latvia. Almost half of the country has forests. There are small lakes and swamps throughout the land.

About half of Latvia's people are Latvians. They have their own culture and language. The Latvian language is one of the oldest in Europe. Other people in Latvia include Russians, Lithuanians, Jews, and Poles.

The people of Latvia like folklore, especially folk songs. They enjoy song festivals, opera, drama, and dance. For special times, they dress in colorful clothing of red, white, and gold. But most of the time, they dress in modern clothes. Most people belong to the Lutheran, Roman Catholic, or Russian Orthodox church.

Riga is the capital of Latvia and its largest city. Many people there work on ships, can food, and make machinery and other products.

For more than 1,000 years, Latvia was ruled by different countries. They included Russia, Lithuania, Poland, Sweden, and the Soviet Union. Latvia won its independence from the Soviet Union in September 1991, and the Soviet Union broke apart later that year.

Facts About Latvia

Capital: Riga.

Area: 24,942 sq. mi. (64,600 km²).

Population: Estimated 1998 population: 2,504,000.

Official language: Latvian.

Climate: Cold winters and mild summers, with 20 to 31 in. (51 to 80 cm) of rainfall a year.

Chief products:

Agriculture: barley, dairy cattle, flax, hogs, oats, potatoes, sugar beets.

Manufacturing: cloth and clothing, processed foods, transportation equipment, wood products.

Form of government: Republic.

Flag

Latvia and its neighbors

Laurier, Sir Wilfrid

Sir Wilfrid Laurier

Sir Wilfrid Laurier (*WIHL frihd LAW rih ay*) (1841-1919) was prime minister of Canada, or Canada's head of government, from 1896 to 1911. He was the first French Canadian to become a prime minister. Queen Victoria of Great Britain knighted Laurier, or made him Sir Wilfrid, in 1897.

Laurier spoke both English and French very well. He was known for his great speeches.

Wilfrid Laurier was born on November 20, 1841, in St. Lin (now Laurentides), Quebec. He studied law at McGill University in Montreal. Laurier graduated in 1864.

After graduation, Laurier became a successful lawyer in Quebec. He was elected to the Quebec legislature, or lawmaking group, in 1871. Three years later, he was elected to the Canadian Parliament, or government. Laurier served in Parliament for a total of 45 years. He was leader of the Liberal Party for 32 years.

Laurier worked to settle conflicts between the French-speaking and English-speaking Canadians. He also tried to make Canada more independent from Great Britain. At that time, Canada was part of Great Britain.

Laurier became prime minister on July 11, 1896. In 1905, during Laurier's term as prime minister, Alberta and Saskatchewan became Canadian provinces. Laurier's government helped many people from different countries settle in the prairies of the new provinces.

In 1911, the Conservative Party gained control of the government. Sir Wilfrid Laurier continued to serve as leader of the Liberal Party. He died on February 17, 1919.

Lava. See Volcano.

Law

• •

The law is the set of rules under which a society lives. No society could exist if people always did whatever they wanted, without thinking about the rights of others. A society also could not exist if people did not understand that there are things they should do for others. The law sets the rules that explain a person's rights—the fair treatment that a person deserves. The law also spells out a person's duties toward others.

The law sets punishments for people who do not follow its rules. Most societies use police, courts, and other government bodies to make sure that people obey the law.

There are two main types of law: public law and private law. Public law explains the rights and duties people have as members of society and as citizens. It includes laws dealing with crimes, such as robbery, and laws about taxes and the government. A constitution—a written set of rules saying what the government can or cannot do—is also public law. Private law, also called civil law, sets the rights and duties people have in their dealings with others. Such dealings include borrowing or lending money, buying a home, settling a divorce, or running a business.

Each country sets its own laws, and so the laws may be different from one place to another. But in many societies, governments try to make the laws fair to all people.

The earliest known set of written laws was developed about 4,100 years ago in the ancient Middle Eastern land of Babylonia, in what is now southeastern Iraq. The ancient Greeks began to develop laws about 2,600 years ago. The ancient Romans began writing laws about 2,450 years ago. Many later laws of Europe were based in part on Roman law.

The King's Bench was England's chief criminal court about 500 years ago. It helped make sure that English people obeyed the same laws no matter where in England they lived.

Lawyers give advice to people who need help with the law. This group of lawyers provides free help for people who need lawyers to represent them in court.

A Book of Leaves

Do you like to collect leaves? You can make them into a book.

Collect many types of leaves on different days and from different places. You can use an encyclopedia or a book about trees to find out what kind of tree they came from.

Press the leaves between sheets of newspaper. Weigh them down with a book so that they dry flat.

Pull the plastic back a page at a time. Arrange two or three leaves on the page. Glue the leaves to the page, press gently with your hands, and let the glue dry. Label each leaf with the name of the tree from which it came. Carefully fold the plastic back over the leaves. Now you can flip through the album and enjoy the beautiful leaves at any time of the year.

Things You Need
- leaves
- newspaper
- photo album with plastic-covered cardboard pages

Lead

Lead (*lehd*) is a soft, heavy, bluish-gray metal. It can be hammered easily into different shapes. It does not rust and is not harmed by powerful chemicals. Lead has been used as a building material and to make pottery for thousands of years.

Lead and lead ore

People use lead in batteries, paints, insect poisons, glass, and other products. Lead also stops X rays. It is used as a shield in rooms with X-ray machines.

People get lead from an ore, or mineral, that is mined underground. But people use much more lead than they mine each year. Much of it comes from recycling, or reusing, the lead in old batteries.

Too much contact with lead can be dangerous. Breathing too much lead dust or fumes, or eating bits of lead, can cause lead poisoning, a serious illness.

Leaf

A leaf is the main food-making part of almost all plants. Leaves come in many different shapes. Many are oval, but others are shaped like arrowheads, feathers, hands, hearts, and countless other objects. Leaves may be flat or thick. Some leaves look like thick sewing needles. The number of leaves on plants ranges from several to thousands.

Most leaves are 1 to 12 inches (2.5 to 30 centimeters) long. But some leaves are huge. The largest leaves grow on the African raffia (*RAF ee uh*) palm. The leaves of this tree grow up to 65 feet (20 meters) long. And some plants have tiny leaves. The leaves of asparagus plants are so tiny that they are hard to see without a magnifying glass.

The importance of leaves

Leaves are important to people. They are eaten as food and used to flavor foods and make such drinks as tea. Some drugs come from leaves. People use certain leaves to make rope. Leaves also help make the air that we breathe. When leaves make the plant's food, they give off a gas called oxygen. People and other animals must breathe oxygen to live.

A leaf makes its food out of energy from sunlight, water from the soil, and carbon dioxide, a gas in the air. This food-making process is called photosynthesis (*FOH tuh SIHN thuh sihs*). Plants need food to grow. Plants also use food to produce flowers and seeds. They store the food made by leaves in their fruits, roots, seeds, stems, and even in the leaves themselves.

Some leaves have special jobs other than making food. The spines of a cactus keep animals from eating the plant. The fat leaves on a tulip bulb store food underground in winter. Many plants that grow in dry places have thick leaves that store water. Tendrils are special leaves that hold climbing plants in place. Some leaves attract, trap, and digest insects.

The life of a leaf

A leaf begins its life in a bud. Buds are the growing parts of a stem. They form along the sides and at the tip of the stem. The bud contains a tightly packed group of very tiny leaves. These leaves unfold and make food for the plant.

The leaf is green because it contains a green substance called chlorophyll (*KLAWR uh fihl*). Chlorophyll helps the leaf make food. The leaf also has other colors, but they are hidden by the

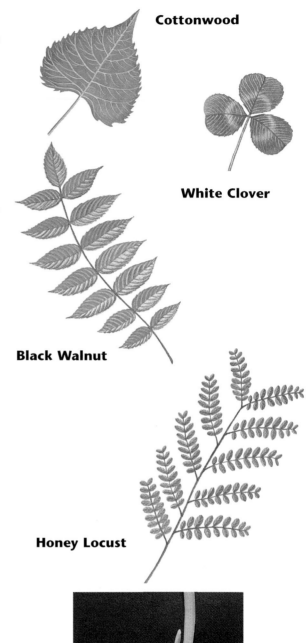

Cottonwood

White Clover

Black Walnut

Honey Locust

A tulip bulb's fat leaves store food underground in winter.

How leaves develop on a lilac bush:
First, leaves form inside a bud. Then, the bud opens. Next, the young leaves unfold. Then, a twig develops.

green. In cool weather, the green color disappears. The leaf may then show its other colors, such as yellow or orange-red. Some dying leaves turn red and purple. When the leaf dies, it dries up and drops to the ground.

On the ground, the dead leaf becomes part of the soil. It then helps provide nourishment for new plant growth.

Other articles to read: **Chlorophyll; Photosynthesis.**

Leaning Tower of Pisa

The Leaning Tower of Pisa is a bell tower in Pisa, Italy. It leans because it was built on soil that was not firm. The tower has eight floors. Each floor has arches all the way around it. A staircase on the inside leads to the top.

The tower is one of three buildings that make up the cathedral of Pisa. These buildings are known for their colorful marble and beautiful arches.

People began building the tower more than 800 years ago and finished it almost 200 years later. After the first three floors were built, the tower began to sink and lean over.

Each year, the tower has leaned a little more. In 1990, the tower was closed for repairs. Engineers are working on the tower's foundation, or base. They hope to straighten the tower enough to keep it from falling.

The Leaning Tower of Pisa

Leather

● ●

Leather is a strong material made from the skin of animals. Most leather comes from cattle hides. But the thinner skins of deer, goats, pigs, and sheep are also widely used. Fancy leathers are made from alligator, shark, and snake hides.

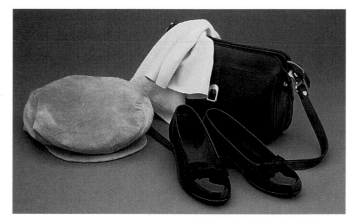

Different types of leather are used to make different products.

Leather is strong, and it lasts a long time. It can be made as soft as cloth or as stiff as wood. Some kinds of leather are thick and heavy, but others are thin. Leather can be dyed in different colors or polished until it is shiny.

Many things that people use every day are made of leather. They include shoes, belts, gloves, jackets, pants, shirts, and purses. Leather is also used to make baseballs, basketballs, and footballs. Most leather is made into shoes.

There are four main kinds of leather: shoe sole leather, shoe upper leather, chamois (*SHAM ee*), and suede (*swayd*). Shoe sole leather is made from the thick skins of cattle and other large animals. Shoe upper leather is produced from the thinner skins of calves and other smaller animals. Some people split thick hides into thin layers.

Most chamois leather is made from split sheepskin. It is as soft as cloth and soaks up water like cloth does. Chamois leather is good for washing and polishing things.

Suede is made from the inside of a cow's skin. Suede is soft and warm. It is used to make clothing and the tops of shoes.

People have used leather since prehistoric times. The process of turning animal skin to leather is called tanning.

Lebanon

Lebanon (*LEHB uh nuhn*) is a small country in western Asia. It lies at the eastern end of the Mediterranean Sea. Israel lies to the south, and Syria lies to the north and east. Beirut, the capital and largest city of Lebanon, is on the coast. About half of Lebanon's people live in the Beirut area.

Lebanon and its neighbors

Land. Sandy beaches stretch along the Mediterranean coast. East of the coast, farmers raise fruit on a narrow plain. Most of Lebanon's cities are in this area.

Rugged mountains rise east of the plain. They extend down most of the length of the country. Farmers raise fruit in the mountains. Mountains also run along the country's eastern border.

A valley lies between the two mountain ranges. Many vegetables are grown there. The ruins of several ancient cities also are in this valley.

People. Most of Lebanon's people are Arabs. A large number are Palestinian Arabs, who once lived on land that is now part of Israel. Many of them came to Lebanon during the wars between Arabs and Israelis. Other groups in Lebanon include Kurds, people of a mountainous region of southwest Asia, and Armenians. Almost all Lebanese speak Arabic, the national language.

More than half of the people of Lebanon are Muslims. They follow the religion of Islam. Almost all the rest are Christians.

Resources and products. A war between Christians and Muslims in the 1970's and more fighting in the 1980's hurt Lebanon's industries and closed many businesses. Many people had no work.

Today, many people work in service industries. They work in banks, stores, hospitals, and hotels. Many people also work in factories and on farms.

History. People have lived in what is now Lebanon for thousands of years. About 4,000 years ago, the Phoenicians (*fih NEE shuhns*) lived in cities along the coast. They were sailors, traders, and explorers. The Roman Empire gained control of the area a little over 2,000 years ago. Ruins of Roman temples and a Roman town still stand in Lebanon.

Christianity came to Lebanon about 1,700 years ago. Many Lebanese became Christians. In the early 600's, Muslims came to Lebanon. Many people along the coast became Muslims. But most people in the mountains remained Christians.

The Ottoman Turks took over Lebanon in 1516. They ruled until World War I (1914-1918), when Britain and France took control of the country.

France helped set up Lebanon's government. The country became independent in 1943. Christian and Muslim leaders agreed to share power in the government.

In the mid-1970's, fights between Christians and Muslims led to civil war. The war ended in 1976. But fighting between Christians, Muslims, and other groups in Lebanon continued. The fighting caused many deaths and destroyed much of Lebanon. A peace plan ended most of the fighting in 1991.

Facts About Lebanon

Capital: Beirut.

Area: 4,015 sq. mi. (10,400 km²).

Population: Estimated 1998 population—3,173,000.

Official language: Arabic.

Climate: Coast—warm, humid summers and mild winters. Mountains—cooler and less humid than coast, but greater rainfall. Valley between mountains—less rainfall than mountains.

Chief products:

Agriculture: apples, cherries, cucumbers, grapes, lemons, oranges, peaches, sugar beets, tomatoes.

Manufacturing: cement, chemicals, cloth, electric appliances, furniture, processed foods.

Form of government: Republic.

Shepherds and their flock at Mt. Lebanon

Flag

Lee, Robert E.

● ●

Robert E. Lee

Robert E. Lee (1807-1870) was a great general. He commanded the Confederate Army of the South during the Civil War (1861-1865). He is one of the best-loved figures in American history.

Robert E. Lee was born near Montross, Virginia, on January 19, 1807. He graduated from the U.S. Military Academy at West Point in 1829 and served as an engineer in the Army. He helped to lay out the boundary line between Ohio and Michigan. Later, he was superintendent of West Point for three years. Then he served in Texas.

In 1861, Texas, Lee's home state of Virginia, and other Southern States seceded (*suh SEED ed*) from, or left, the United States. The Civil War began that same year. Lee resigned from the U.S. Army to defend Virginia, even though he did not want to see the country divided.

Lee took command of the Army of Northern Virginia. His job was almost impossible, but he won several important battles. In July 1863, his soldiers fought at Gettysburg, Pennsylvania. After three days of bitter fighting, they lost.

Early in 1865, Lee was made chief of all the Confederate armies. His troops were tired and hungry. They had to retreat. Lee surrendered to General Ulysses S. Grant of the Union, or northern, Army on April 9, 1865, at Appomattox, Virginia.

Lee spent his last years as president of Washington College, now Washington and Lee University. His home has been preserved in Arlington National Cemetery, near Washington, D.C.

Other articles to read: **Civil War.**

Traveller was the horse Lee rode throughout the Civil War.

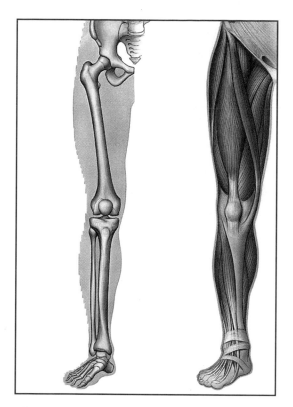

The leg contains large, strong bones, *left,* and powerful muscles, *right.*

Leg

Legs are parts that support the bodies of people or animals. They are used to stand and move.

In people, the thigh has the longest, strongest bone in the body. The lower leg has two long bones. The largest one is the shinbone. The knee joint is like a hinge between the thigh bone and lower leg bones. A small bone called the kneecap is in front of the knee joint.

Muscles are attached to the bones. In the front of the thigh, a big muscle straightens the knee and bends the thigh at the hip. Muscles in the back of the thigh bend the knee and straighten the thigh.

Muscles in the lower leg bend and straighten the ankles and toes. They also bend the foot sideways.

Other articles to read: **Foot; Human body; Muscle.**

Lemon

Lemons are small fruits. They belong to a group called citrus fruits, which also include limes and oranges. Lemons are oval and have a yellow rind, or peel. Most lemons taste sour, so people rarely eat fresh lemons.

Lemons are used to flavor soft drinks, desserts, and many other foods. Cooks use lemon juice and oil from the lemon rind to flavor meat and fish. Lemon oil is also used as a scent.

Lemon trees grow up to 25 feet (7.6 meters) tall. They have thorns, pointed leaves, and sweet-smelling white blossoms. The trees often have flowers and fruit at the same time.

Lemon trees can be damaged by freezing weather. Growers use heaters, big fans, or water sprays to help protect the trees from cold.

Lemon

Lemur

• •

Lemurs (*LEE muhrz*) are long-tailed animals with fluffy fur. Lemurs are mammals, animals that feed their young with the mother's milk. They belong to the group of mammals called primates, which also includes monkeys, apes, and humans.

Lemurs live only in Madagascar and Comoros. Both countries are islands off the coast of Africa. The smallest lemurs—lesser mouse lemurs—look like furry mice. Ring-tailed lemurs are gray on top and white underneath. They look like monkeys with a pointed nose. Their tails have rings of black and white fur. Ruffed lemurs are usually a mixture of black and white with a fluffy white ruff, or collar.

Lemurs have few enemies on the islands where they live. Still, many kinds are in danger of dying out, because people have cut down the forests where they make their homes.

Ring-tailed lemur

Lens

• •

A lens is a piece of curved glass, plastic, or some other see-through material. Lenses may be used to make objects look bigger or smaller. Lenses may also be used to make what we see look sharp and clear. There are two main kinds of lenses, convex and concave. Convex lenses are curved out, and concave lenses are curved in. Lenses are an important part of binoculars, cameras, microscopes, telescopes, and many other devices.

The lens is also an important part of the human eye. Our lenses help our eyes make sharp pictures of objects that are near or far. When people have blurry eyesight, they wear eyeglasses with glass or plastic lenses to correct the problem. Sometimes they wear contact lenses on the eyes.

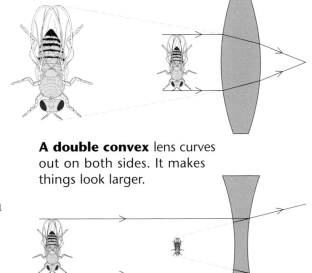

A double convex lens curves out on both sides. It makes things look larger.

A double concave lens curves in on both sides. It makes things look smaller.

Leonardo da Vinci

• •

Leonardo da Vinci (*lee uh NAHR doh duh VIHN chee*) (1452-1519) was one of the greatest painters in history. He was gifted in many other ways as well. Leonardo was one of the most important people in the Renaissance (*REHN uh sahns*). The Renaissance was a time when the importance of arts, sciences, and many kinds of learning grew very rapidly.

Mona Lisa

Leonardo was probably born outside the village of Vinci, near Florence, Italy. His name, *da Vinci,* means *from Vinci.* He studied with Andrea del Verrocchio, a leading painter and sculptor in Florence, and then worked for him.

Leonardo da Vinci's self portrait

Leonardo had his own studio in Florence for several years. Then he went to Milan to become an artist in a duke's court. While he was there, he also worked as an engineer. He designed forts, weapons, locks for Milan's canals, and stages for shows. He also painted his first important work, *Madonna of the Rocks* (about 1483). He painted *The Last Supper,* a religious picture of Jesus and his apostles, around 1497.

In 1499, the French overthrew the duke. Leonardo returned to Florence. His work in Milan had gained people's respect. He was hired to do a large battle painting. While he worked on it, he painted the *Mona Lisa,* a picture of a young woman. The battle painting no longer exists, but the *Mona Lisa* is probably the most famous painting of a person ever created.

In Leonardo's later years, King Francis I of France invited Leonardo to become his royal painter, engineer, and architect. Leonardo spent his last three years in France.

In his work, Leonardo looked at things carefully and made many drawings. He studied the human body and the bodies of animals. He also studied plants, the stars and planets, and many other science subjects. Leonardo planned to write books on the subjects, but he never finished them. He kept notebooks full of drawings, ideas he had written down, and plans for inventions such as flying machines and a helicopter. His notebooks were published nearly 400 years after he died.

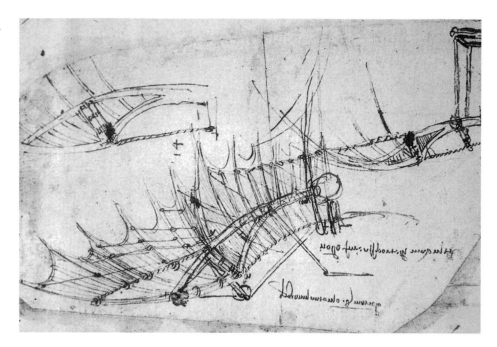

Leonardo kept notebooks full of drawings and ideas for inventions. These sketches are a plan for winged flight.

Leopard

● ●

Leopards (*LEHP uhrdz*) are large animals in the cat family. The leopard is the third-largest cat in Asia and Africa. Only tigers and lions are larger. The biggest male leopards are almost 9 feet (2.7 meters) long from nose to tail.

Most leopards have light tan fur with black spots. Leopards that live in forests are darker. Black leopards are so dark that the spots are hard to see.

Leopards are fierce hunters. They kill and feed on such animals as monkeys, antelope, peacocks, snakes, and goats. They are good climbers and often carry the animals they kill up a tree. Females have two to four cubs at a time.

Leopards have been hunted for their beautiful fur. They are now disappearing in many places.

Leopard

Lesotho

● ●

Lesotho (*lay SOO too*) is a mountainous country in Africa. It is surrounded by the Republic of South Africa. Lesotho is about 200 miles (320 kilometers) from the Indian Ocean. Maseru (*MAZ uh ROO*) is the capital and largest city.

Most of Lesotho's people are African people called Basotho or Basuto. They live in villages and raise crops on nearby land. The people own all the land together, and the chiefs decide where each family will farm. The Basotho also raise animals.

Lesotho is a beautiful country, but it is poor. Too much farming has worn out the soil. There are not enough jobs for everyone, so many men go to South Africa to work. Factories in Lesotho make clothing, furniture, and processed food. The country has some diamonds that could be mined.

In the late 1700's and early 1800's, wars between African peoples broke out. Some groups escaped into the area that is now Lesotho, where they were protected by a strong chief named Moshoeshoe. Both the British and Dutch settlers fought Moshoeshoe's people. Finally, Moshoeshoe asked Britain for help. The area came under Britain's control. It was called Basutoland. Basutoland became the independent kingdom of Lesotho in 1966.

Facts About Lesotho

Capital: Maseru.

Area: 11,720 sq. mi. (30,355 km²).

Population: Estimated 1998 population—2,216,000.

Official languages: English and Sesotho.

Climate: Mild, moist. Highlands have some freezing temperatures and snow in winter.

Chief products:

Agriculture: beans, cattle, corn, goats, mohair, peas, sheep, sorghum, wheat, wool.

Form of government: Constitutional monarchy.

Flag

Lesotho and its neighbors

Boston lettuce

Iceberg lettuce

Romaine lettuce

Leaf lettuce

Bibb lettuce

Celtuce lettuce

An Indian named Sacagawea helped guide Lewis and Clark.

Lettuce

Lettuce is a leafy green vegetable. It usually grows close to the ground. It is used mainly in salads, and most people eat it raw. It is a very healthful food.

There are three main kinds of lettuce. Head lettuce is the most common. Its leaves curl around the center and form a ball shape. Leaf lettuce grows in thick, leafy clumps instead of heads. Gardeners grow more leaf lettuce than any other kind. Romaine lettuce grows long and upright. The leaves curl inward. Romaine contains more vitamins and minerals than any other kind of lettuce.

Most lettuce is planted right in the ground, but some lettuce is started in buildings called greenhouses. Plants in greenhouses get enough light and water and are protected from cold. Lettuce must be packed, cooled, and shipped right after harvesting because it spoils easily.

Lewis and Clark expedition

Lewis and Clark were explorers who led an important expedition. They traveled through what is now the Northwestern United States.

Meriwether Lewis (1774-1809) was a captain in the United States Army. President Thomas Jefferson asked him to plan the journey. Lewis asked William Clark (1770-1838), a former officer, to join him.

Lewis and Clark started out from St. Louis, Missouri, in May 1804. They traveled up the Missouri River, across the Rocky Mountains, and along the Columbia and other rivers to the Pacific Ocean. They returned in September 1806, after

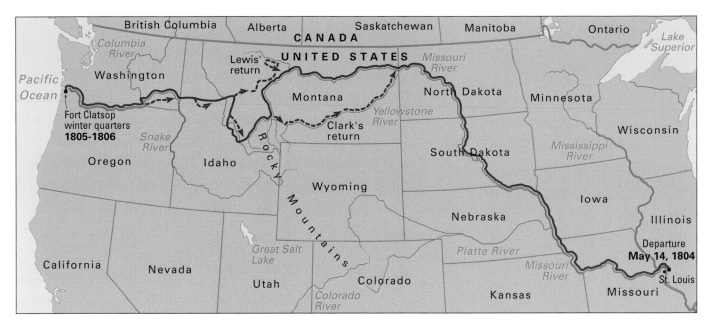

Lewis and Clark's route took them from St. Louis to the Pacific Ocean and back. When they returned to St. Louis in 1806, they brought with them valuable information about the new frontier.

traveling about 8,000 miles (12,800 kilometers). They brought back maps and information about plants, animals, minerals, and American Indians. The United States then claimed the land that is now Oregon, Washington, and Idaho.

Other articles to read: **Sacagawea.**

Lewis, C. S.

●●●●●●●●●●●●●●●●●●●●●●●

C. S. Lewis (1898-1963) was a British author. He is known for his clever and amusing stories. Lewis wrote more than 30 books, including children's stories, science fiction, and books on religion. Most of his writings teach lessons about right and wrong.

Clive Staples Lewis was born in Belfast, Northern Ireland. As an adult, he taught literature, the study of writings, at both Oxford and Cambridge universities in England. Between 1950 and 1956, he wrote a popular series of children's books called *The Chronicles of Narnia.* His other books include *Out of the Silent Planet* (1938), about three scientists who travel to Mars.

C. S. Lewis

Liberia

Flag

Liberia is a country in west Africa. It is bordered by Sierra Leone on the northwest, Guinea on the northeast, Ivory Coast on the east, and the Atlantic Ocean on the west. Monrovia (*muhn ROH vee uh*) is the capital and largest city. Liberia has a rugged coastline. Away from the ocean, the land is higher, with low hills.

Most Liberians are Africans. Some of them are people whose families came from the United States more than 150 years ago. In the early 1800's, a group of people in the United States bought land along the coast. Some African slaves in the United States had been freed. The group sent them to settle there. Other Liberians come from families who have always lived in Africa. They include Kpelle and Bassa people.

Many Liberians farm for a living. People in cities work in schools, stores, factories, and offices. Liberia has iron ore, and some people work in mining.

Liberia's earliest people were from eastern Africa. Portuguese explorers began to trade with people along the coast in the 1400's.

In 1847, Liberia became independent. It was a poor country. Most of the power belonged to the people whose families had come from the United States. War broke out in 1989 between various groups. In 1996, the people agreed to stop fighting and try to start a new government. Elections were held in 1997.

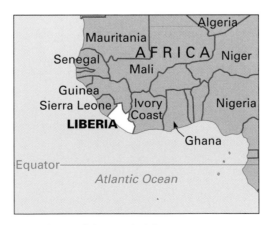

Liberia and its neighbors

Liberty Bell

● ● ● ● ● ● ● ● ● ● ● ● ● ● ● ● ● ●

The Liberty Bell is a symbol (*SIHM buhl*) of independence in the United States. It was brought from England to Philadelphia in 1753. It rang to mark special events and to call people together. One event was on July 8, 1776, to announce the adoption of the Declaration of Independence. The Declaration of Independence was signed on July 4, 1776. In 1841, the bell cracked.

Until 1976, the Liberty Bell was kept in Independence Hall in Philadelphia. It now hangs nearby, in the Liberty Bell Pavilion, but the bell is no longer rung. However, it is struck like a gong on important days and the sound is broadcast so that everyone can hear it.

Liberty, Statue of.

See **Statue of Liberty**.

The Liberty Bell

Library

A library is a collection of many kinds of information. A library has books, magazines, newspapers, videos, films, computer programs, and recordings. In a library, people can learn about history, science, art, and government. They can also go to the library to listen to a story, watch a film, see works of art, or listen to music. There are special libraries in universities and law offices, in hospitals, and in schools.

At the library, students can select books on subjects that interest them.

Public libraries

Public libraries serve all the people in a community, town, or city, including children. The children's librarian tries to make the children's part of the library a friendly place with colorful posters and interesting exhibits and displays. Tables, chairs, and shelves are set up in a special way for children. Children's librarians plan programs for many interests and age levels. They enjoy reading stories to children at story hours.

Librarians also help young people and adults learn about different jobs or careers. Sometimes librarians meet with groups to talk about books. People of all ages can find information and learn

Many libraries have comfortable lounges for people to read and study.

Readers use computers at a library to look for books. They also use computers to look for information on CD-ROM's and on the Internet.

about community activities in a public library.

Public libraries also serve people with special needs and interests. Sometimes libraries buy books in different languages, or books on tape for people who can't see well. Sometimes they show the work of artists who live in the area. Sometimes they have neighborhood or visiting poets read their works. Many public libraries have classes to help people learn English or how to read.

Some cities have branch libraries. Then everyone in the city has a small library nearby. Some cities have bookmobiles. These are vans that stop at various places around the city to lend books. The books from public libraries usually cost nothing to borrow.

A bookmobile brings books to people who live far from a library.

School libraries

Many schools have libraries. School libraries have materials that help children do their schoolwork or find out more about their special interests. Some school libraries have interesting objects to examine, such as birds' nests, musical instruments, maps, and games. Some have computers and videos.

A school library helps teachers, too. For example, if a second-grade class is studying Mexico, the teacher can borrow photographs of Mexican life and compact discs (CD's) of Mexican music from the school library. Students may work together in small groups in the library, watching videos or discussing questions. Sometimes older students help younger students in the school library by reading aloud to them or helping them learn to write.

Special materials can often be found in libraries. These students are studying art books and photos of famous paintings for a school project.

The children's section of a public library has books, furniture, and special programs for younger readers.

Special libraries offer certain kinds of material. This library has thousands of maps for people to study.

Challenges and problems

Librarians must take good care of books and find ways to handle them when they get old. Over time, paper crumbles. Librarians know how to repair old books. Sometimes they copy them onto film to save important information from the past.

One problem that libraries sometimes face is censorship. Censorship means that certain books or other materials are not allowed in the library. Some people object to books about religion, sex, or government, or books that have bad language. Other people think that all types of books should be in libraries. Librarians must listen to everyone and then decide what books to buy for the library.

Another problem that libraries have is theft, or stealing. Each year, books are stolen from the library. Libraries use different ways to check books that are going out. Sometimes a guard makes sure that people have checked out a book before they leave the library with it. Some libraries have a system that rings an alarm if a person tries to leave the library with material that was not checked out.

Libraries have money problems, too. They must ask for money from the government and from other groups. They must figure out how much money they have and how much they can spend. Librarians must decide what books are best to buy and what services people need most.

Using the library

Most libraries have two sections of books and other materials. Books in the reference section, such as dictionaries and encyclopedias, must be used in the library. People cannot take reference books home. Most other books can be checked out and taken home if you have a library card. It is easy to get a library card. The librarian will help you fill out a form to get one.

Librarians give every item in the library a special number called a call number. Call numbers help you find books and other materials. They tell you where the item is in the library. You can get the call number from the library computer. You can look for books by author, title, or subject on the computer.

Or you can just walk around and look at the books on the shelves. Often, you find interesting books to read just by taking books off the shelves or by looking at the book jackets and book posters on the library walls. You can also ask the librarian to suggest a book about something that interests you, such as horses, mysteries, or jokes.

History of libraries

Libraries have been around as long as writing itself—about 5,500 years. At first, books were made of such materials as clay, bones, metal, wax, wood, plants, silk, and leather. Writings on clay tablets were found in Mesopotamia, a long-ago society that once was where Turkey and Iraq are today.

Libraries in ancient Egypt, Greece, and Rome had books written on paper that was made from a plant called papyrus. Then the paper was rolled up into tubes called scrolls. The most famous library of ancient times was the Alexandrian Library in Egypt. That library had more than 400,000 scrolls, including scrolls of writings from the Bible.

Most early libraries in colonial America belonged to ministers. Most of the books in these early libraries were about religion, medicine, and animals. Later, people could pay to belong to a library. Free libraries became popular in the 1830's. In the 1880's Andrew Carnegie, a Scottish-born American, gave millions of dollars to build more than 2,500 public libraries throughout the world.

Other articles to read: **Book; Literature for children; Magazine; Motion picture; Newspaper; Printing.**

This clay tablet was probably from a royal library in Mesopotamia. It is about 2,600 years old.

The Alexandrian Library was the most famous library of ancient times. This picture shows how it might have looked.

Libya

Facts About Libya

Capital: Tripoli.

Area: 679,362 sq. mi. (1,759,540 km²).

Population: Estimated 1998 population—5,965,000.

Official language: Arabic.

Climate: Mild along the coast, with light rainfall. Extremely hot in the desert, with cool nights and almost no rain.

Chief products:

Agriculture: barley, cattle, chickens, citrus fruits, dates, olives, potatoes, sheep, tomatoes, wheat.

Manufacturing: cement, oil, processed foods.

Mining: oil.

Form of government: Islamic socialist state.

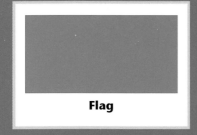

Flag

Libya is a country in northern Africa, on the coast of the Mediterranean Sea. It is bordered by Egypt and Sudan on the east, Chad and Niger on the south, and Algeria and Tunisia on the west. Tripoli (*TRIHP uh lee*) is Libya's capital and largest city.

Most of Libya's people are a mixture of Arab and Berber peoples. The Berbers lived in the area long before the Arabs arrived. Almost all Libyans follow the religion of Islam.

The Sahara, a huge desert, covers most of Libya. A few people live in desert oases, areas where there is water. However, most Libyans live near the Mediterranean coast.

Only a small amount of land is good for farming, so Libya must buy most of its food. The country is rich in oil. Most of Libya's money comes from selling oil to other countries. People use oil for running machines and other purposes.

People have lived in what is now Libya for thousands of years. Arabs spread the Islamic religion to the area in the 600's. In the 1500's, most of Libya became part of the Ottoman Empire, which was based in Turkey. In the early and middle 1900's, Italy and Britain controlled parts of Libya. Britain and France took control from Italy during World War II (1939-1945), with the help of Muslim forces from Libya.

Libya and its neighbors

Libya became an independent kingdom in 1951. In 1959, oil was discovered. Libya became wealthy, but few people shared the wealth. In September 1969, a group of military officers took over the country's government. Colonel Muammar Muhammad al-Qadhafi took power.

Lice. See **Louse.**

Liechtenstein

• •

Liechtenstein (*LIHK tuhn STYN*) is one of the world's smallest countries. It lies in central Europe. Liechtenstein is bordered by Switzerland and Austria. Vaduz (*VAH doots*) is the capital city.

The people of Liechtenstein come from a German group that settled in the area more than 1,500 years ago. They have many close ties with Switzerland.

The Rhine River flows along the western border of Liechtenstein. A narrow strip of farmland lies next to the river. Mountains cover most of the country's eastern and southern sections.

Until about 50 years ago, most people in Liechtenstein were farmers. Now the country has many industries. Metal products, electronic equipment, and medicines are some important products. Also, collectors around the world buy the country's beautiful postage stamps. Many farmers in Liechtenstein raise such crops as wheat and grapes, while other farmers raise cattle.

Liechtenstein was once two small states. A prince from Vienna, Austria, named Johann-Adam Liechtenstein became the ruler of one of the states in 1699 and of the other in 1712. His family has ruled Liechtenstein ever since.

Liechtenstein has been independent since 1712, except for a short time in the early 1800's. In 1924, the country agreed to join Switzerland in some of its services. The people use Swiss money, and Switzerland runs Liechtenstein's postal system and telephone service. Switzerland also handles some of Liechtenstein's trade agreements with other countries.

Facts About Liechtenstein

Capital: Vaduz.

Area: 62 sq. mi. (160 km²).

Population: Estimated 1998 population—31,000.

Official language: German.

Climate: Mild.

Chief products:

Agriculture: beef and dairy cattle, fruits and vegetables, wheat.

Manufacturing: ceramics, electronic equipment, heating appliances, medicine, metal products.

Form of government: Constitutional monarchy.

Flag

Liechtenstein and its neighbors

Life

Life makes people, plants, and animals living things. Such things as stones, houses, and cars do not have life, and are not living things.

There are more than 10 million kinds of living things. Some, like bacteria, are too small to see. Others, like blue whales and redwood trees, are huge. Living things are found in many places, but they are all alike in some ways.

What living things do

Living things can reproduce. They can make more of their own kind of living thing. Some living things, such as bacteria, reproduce by dividing in two. Most plants and animals reproduce by combining material from a male and a female.

Living things grow. Many plants grow by taking in chemicals from the air and water. Animals grow by eating plants or other animals.

Living things must use energy to live. They break down the chemicals in food to get some of the energy. Green plants also get energy from the sun.

Most living things move. In some living things, such as plants, much of the movement is inside. Animals may move in ways that are easier to see.

Living things can sense changes around themselves and react in some way. Often, they move. For example, a turtle pulls into its shell, and a plant grows toward the sun.

Living things can change to survive (keep on living). Over many years, they may become able to eat new foods or live in hotter, colder, wetter, or dryer places.

Living things grow. Usually they become larger. They may change in other ways, too.

Living things reproduce. They make more of their own kind of living thing.

What living things are made of

All living things are made up of tiny parts called cells (*SELZ*). The simplest living things have only one cell. Large living things, such as a dog, a tree, or a person, have many parts. So, they have billions of cells.

Each cell has a thin covering called a membrane (*MEHM brayn*). It separates the cell from other cells. Only certain substances can pass through it. Inside, most cells have a jellylike outer part and a center called a nucleus (*NOO klee uhs*). The nucleus is the control center. It tells the cell what to do.

Large living things have several different kinds of cells. Cells that work in the same way form tissues (*TISH ooz*), such as muscle. Several kinds of tissue form the body's organs, such as the heart, liver, and brain.

Living things sense changes. When they do, they act in certain ways. This plant turns toward the sun when it senses sunlight.

How life began

The religions of many people have stories of how living things came to be. In the Christian religion, the Bible tells how God created the earth and all living things.

Living things use energy. Plants make food by using the sun's energy. Animals eat plants or other animals.

Scientists have theories (*THEE uhr eez*), or ideas, about how life began. Long ago, some scientists thought that tiny cells floated to the earth from outer space. Most scientists today think life was created from chemicals here on the earth. Scientists are doing experiments to learn how that could have happened.

Most living things move. It is easy to see many animals move. In some living things, most of the movement is inside.

Other articles to read: **Adaptation; Biology; Cell; Creationism; Death; Evolution; Life cycle; Reproduction; Reproduction, human.**

Life cycle

● ●

A life cycle is a set of steps, or stages, that living things go through as they grow, change, and produce other living things. The life cycle starts at a certain point, such as when a queen bee lays eggs. It includes all the steps until a new bee becomes a queen and lays eggs.

In mammals, such as dogs, the life cycle is simple. The new animal develops in the mother's body. It is born and it grows. When it is grown, it reproduces. It becomes the parent of a new animal like itself.

Other articles to read: **Reproduction; Reproduction, human.**

An ant's life cycle has four steps. It begins when the queen lays eggs.

A larva develops from each egg.

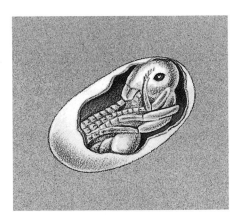

The pupa forms after a few weeks. Inside the pupa, the larva's body changes.

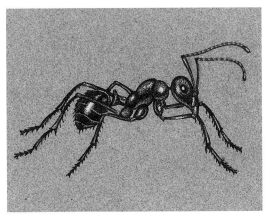

The adult ant comes out of the pupa. An adult queen ant will lay more eggs.

Light

Light is a kind of energy that makes it possible for us to see. Some things, such as the sun and lights in a room, give off light. We see all other things because light bounces off them and travels to us.

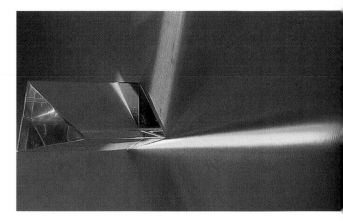

A prism breaks sunlight that passes through it into colors.

How light is made

Some light, such as sunlight, comes from nature. Other light comes from things people make, such as lamps. But all light comes from atoms (*AT uhmz*), tiny particles of matter that make up everything in the universe. Atoms sometimes gain extra energy and give it off as light. Sunlight comes from atoms that give off energy inside the sun.

One way to make atoms give off light is to heat them. A light bulb glows because electricity heats a wire inside it. The heated atoms gain extra energy. They give it off as light.

A few things give off light without being heated very much. Some materials glow in the dark. Some insects and other living things glow.

The nature of light

In some ways, light acts as a wave. It has high and low places, like waves on a pond. Light waves can be long or short. In some ways, light also acts like tiny particles that travel in a straight line.

Sunlight is white light. It is made up of many colors. It can be passed through a piece of glass with a special shape, called a prism (*PRIHZ uhm*). Then it breaks into all the colors we can see, from deep violet, blue, and green through yellow, orange, and red.

The violet waves are the shortest waves we can see, and red waves are the longest. Waves too short to be seen are called ultraviolet rays. They cause sunburn and suntan. Waves too long to be seen are called infrared rays. They cause the warming we feel in sunlight.

A firefly makes its own light. Organs in its body contain chemicals that make it glow without giving off heat.

How light behaves

When light hits an object, it may bounce off, or reflect (*rih FLEHKT*). It behaves somewhat like a bouncing ball. If it hits a surface straight, it reflects straight back. But if it hits at an angle, it bounces in another direction.

When light passes through something, such as passing from air through water, it may bend and change its direction.

When light hits an object, the object may soak up some colors and reflect others. The reflected colors—for example, red in a flower—are what we see.

Measuring light

Scientists measure light in many ways. They measure wavelengths. They also measure the brightness of a light. The speed of light in empty space is always the same. In space, light travels at 186,282 miles (299,792 kilometers) per second.

Other articles to read: **Color; Edison, Thomas Alva; Electricity; Prism; Rainbow; Sun.**

Light bounces off the stop sign, the bicycle rider's clothes, and the reflectors on the bike. This helps drivers see the rider and the sign as it gets dark.

HANDS-ON!

Play Light Ray Tag

You don't need lasers to play a light ray game. Use sunlight instead.

You and your friend should hold your mirrors in the light near the window. The sun's rays will bounce off each mirror and make a spot of light somewhere in the room.

Choose a place, like the middle of the ceiling, to be the "base," a place where a light spot cannot be tagged. The spot can stay on "base" while the player counts to five.

To play the game, you and your friend try to "tag" each other's light spot. Each time one spot tags the other spot, the tagger scores a point.

After five minutes, add up the score. The player with the most points wins.

Things You Need:
• a sunny window
• 2 hand mirrors
• a friend

Lighthouse

Lighthouses are towers with a very strong light. They tell sailors that land is near and warn them of dangerous rocks and reefs. They also help sailors figure out where their ship is.

People build lighthouses on land that sticks out into the ocean, and on rocks that jut out of the sea. Some lighthouses stand in the sea itself. They are built on rocks beneath the water.

Every lighthouse gives off a different pattern of light. Some have a steady light. Others have patterns of long or short flashes. The patterns of light tell the sailors which lighthouse they are seeing. Then they know exactly where they are.

In daytime, sailors can recognize the lighthouse. Lighthouses that look alike are painted with different patterns, such as checks or stripes.

The lamps in a lighthouse shine through lenses. The lenses make the light stronger, so that it can be seen for many miles. Many lighthouses also use foghorns or bells to signal ships in bad weather, when the light is hard to see.

Lighthouses were probably first used by the people of ancient Egypt. At first, they built fires on hilltops. Later, they built towers. The ancient Romans built lighthouses in many places. The first lighthouse in North America was Boston Lighthouse. It was built in 1716.

Today, most lighthouses are automatic. They do not need people to run them. But in the United States, some people still work in lighthouses.

West Quoddy Lighthouse in Lubec, Maine, is painted with stripes so that, during the day, sailors can tell which lighthouse it is.

Drum Point Lighthouse in Solomons, Maryland, sits on a platform. Its light flashes white, then red.

Lightning

During a lightning storm, huge electric sparks jump between clouds or from the clouds to the ground.

Lightning is a giant electric spark. Most of the lightning people see is a spark between the sky and the ground. But lightning also travels within clouds and between clouds. Lightning makes the air in its path so hot that it rushes outward. The air makes a cracking sound that we hear as thunder.

Everything in the world is made up of tiny particles called atoms (*AT uhmz*). Sometimes the atoms in clouds become charged, or filled, with electricity. When charged atoms move toward one another, they create a spark.

The spark travels down from the cloud. When it gets close to the earth, an electric current rushes upward from a tall tree or building to meet it. That electric current makes the lightning that people see. A flash of lightning often has several quick strokes. This makes the lightning seem to flicker.

There are several kinds of lightning, such as forks, streaks, ribbons, chains, and floating balls. Sheet lightning, which lights up the sky, is not a different kind of lightning. It is just too far away for people to see the flash or hear the thunder. Sometimes the lightning is hidden by clouds.

Lightning strikes the earth about 100 times each second. People can be hurt or killed by lightning. During thunderstorms, people are safest in a house or a large building. They should stay away from tall trees, water, high places, and metal things, such as bicycles.

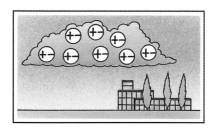

Lightning is electricity that moves between a cloud and the ground. Atoms in the cloud become charged with electricity. There are two kinds of charges: positive (+) and negative (-). Before a storm, *left,* every negative charge is pulled toward a positive charge. During a storm, *right,* the charges are pulled apart. Negative charges from the cloud rush toward positive charges from the ground. They make an electric current, causing lightning.

Lily

● ●

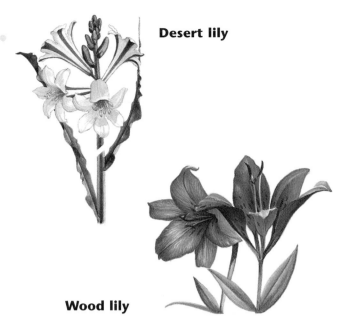

Desert lily

Wood lily

Lilies are flowering plants. They belong to one of the largest, most important plant families. The lily family includes such plants as asparagus and aloe. A few other plants that do not have *lily* as part of their name are in the lily family. These include the sweet-smelling hyacinth. Some plants that do have *lily* in their names, such as the water lily, are not true lilies.

There are more than 4,000 kinds of lilies. They grow from scaly bulbs. Most lily plants have straight stems and bright-colored flowers. The flowers are trumpet-shaped and have six petals.

Lilies grow best in rich, sandy soil that is not too wet. They need to be protected from strong winds and bright sun.

Lincoln, Abraham

● ●

As a boy, Lincoln read by firelight in his family's log cabin. He had little schooling but loved books.

Abraham Lincoln (1809-1865) became the sixteenth president of the United States in 1861. He led the United States during the Civil War (1861-1865).

Lincoln was born in a log cabin near Hodgenville, Kentucky. He went to school for less than a year, but he learned to read, and he loved books. He started a store in New Salem, Illinois, but it failed. He studied law, became a lawyer, and moved to Springfield.

In 1858, Lincoln ran for Congress against Illinois Senator Stephen A. Douglas. He and Douglas debated, or argued, about slavery. In some states, people kept slaves. In others, slavery was against the law. Lincoln said that slavery was evil. He wanted to end slavery. Douglas said that people should vote on whether or not there should be

Abraham Lincoln

slavery. Douglas won the election, but Lincoln became well known.

In 1860, the Republicans ran Lincoln for president. He won easily, but several Southern States left the Union—the United States. The Civil War broke out early in 1861. On January 1, 1863, Lincoln said that slaves in states that had left the Union were free. In 1863, Lincoln also spoke at a battlefield in Gettysburg, Pennsylvania. His short speech, known as Lincoln's Gettysburg Address, became famous.

In 1864, Union troops were winning. Lincoln was elected again. On April 9, 1865, General Robert E. Lee surrendered. The Civil War was over.

On April 14, only five days after the war ended, Lincoln went to see a play. He was shot by John Wilkes Booth, a well-known actor. Lincoln died the following day and was buried in Springfield, Illinois.

Lindbergh, Anne Morrow

Anne Morrow Lindbergh (1906-   ) is an American poet and writer. Her husband was the American aviator (*AY vee ay tuhr*), or pilot, Charles A. Lindbergh.

Anne Morrow was born in Englewood, New Jersey. Her father worked for the United States government. She became a pilot and made many long flights with her husband. She wrote two books about their trips together, *North to the Orient* (1935) and *Listen! The Wind* (1938). Her best-known books are *Gift from the Sea* (1955), about the meaning of a woman's life, and *The Unicorn and Other Poems, 1935-1955* (1956). Other books include *Hour of Gold, Hour of Lead* (1973), and *War Within and Without* (1980).

Other articles to read: **Lindbergh, Charles Augustus.**

Anne Morrow Lindbergh, *right,* with her husband Charles

Lindbergh, Charles Augustus

● ●

Charles Augustus Lindbergh (1902-1974) was an American aviator (*AY vee ay tuhr*), or pilot. He made the first solo, or one-person, nonstop flight across the Atlantic Ocean.

Charles Lindbergh was born in Detroit, Michigan, and grew up in Minnesota. He studied engineering in college, but after two years, he left school to fly. In 1924, he joined the army and trained as a pilot.

A New York businessman had offered $25,000 to the first aviator to fly nonstop from New York to Paris. By 1927, no one had done it. Lindbergh helped design a plane, and a St. Louis businessman helped him pay for it. On May 20, 1927, Lindbergh took off from New York in his plane, *Spirit of St. Louis*. He landed at an airfield near Paris the next day. He had flown more than 3,600 miles (5,790 kilometers) in $33\frac{1}{2}$ hours.

Lindbergh was honored with many awards. In 1929, he and Anne Morrow were married. In 1932, their first child was kidnapped and killed. The Lindberghs moved to Europe and lived there until 1939.

After they returned to the United States, Lindbergh did not believe the United States should enter World War II (1939-1945). He worked to keep the nation from fighting in it, and he resigned from the army. But in 1944, he went to the Pacific war area and flew fighter planes there.

After the war, Lindbergh traveled and lived on the island of Maui, Hawaii. He died there in 1974.

Other articles to read: **Lindbergh, Anne Morrow.**

Charles Lindbergh made the first solo nonstop flight across the Atlantic Ocean in the *Spirit of St. Louis* plane, *above.*

Lion

Lions are big, powerful animals. They are probably the most famous animals in the cat family. Lions are called the "king of beasts" because of their beauty and power.

Lions are very strong. Full-grown male lions are about 9 feet (3 meters) long from nose to tail. They have manes, or long thick hair that covers the head and neck. Females have no manes.

Most lions live on grassy plains in the middle and southern parts of Africa. Their color helps them hide. Their fur is brownish yellow, the same color as dry grass. A few lions live in the Gir Forest in India.

More than any other cats, lions like company. They live together in a group called a pride. Each pride has several grown males, several females, and their cubs (young). Their life is usually quiet. They spend most of the day sleeping or resting. Male cubs are chased away from the pride when they are about 2 years old. In time, some of them take over a pride of their own.

Females have their first cubs when they are 3 or 4 years old. The cubs are born blind and helpless. They live on their mother's milk for the first six weeks. Then they begin eating meat. By the time they are about 2 years old, they hunt for themselves.

Lions hunt to live. They prefer large animals, such as antelope, buffalo, and zebras. Most of the animals they hunt run faster than the lions can. So lions surprise their prey. They creep up on it slowly. Then they rush at it, grab it, and pull it down. Sometimes several lions work together. They circle around an animal and chase it toward other

A pride of lions

Lioness chasing a zebra

lions that are hiding in the grass, waiting for it.

People are a lion's worst enemy. Some people kill lions to protect their farm animals. For hundreds of years, many people have also hunted lions as a sport.

In the Gir Forest of India, people have destroyed areas where lions live by cutting down trees. Africa has many wildlife parks where lions may not be hunted. Most people today would rather photograph lions than shoot them.

Liquid

Liquids are one of the three forms that things can take. The other two forms are solids and gases. Water is a liquid, rock is a solid, and air is a gas.

All these things are made up of matter. The matter is made of tiny particles called molecules (*MAHL uh kyoolz*). The molecules in liquids can flow. They are not locked in place like the molecules in solids. So when liquids are poured into a container, they take the shape of the container.

When liquids are heated or cooled, they can change into gases or solids. For example, when water is heated, it changes into steam. The water molecules mix with the air—a gas. When water is frozen, it turns into ice—a solid.

Other articles to read: **Gas; Matter; Molecule; Solid.**

A liquid takes the shape of the thing that holds it.

Literature for children

Literature (*LIHT uhr uh chur*) for children includes all the stories, poems, and fact books that young readers enjoy. Some of these books are written just for children. Others may be books for grown-ups that children also like.

Pictures are a special part of children's books. And picture books are a special kind of children's book. The pictures, as much as the words, tell the story.

Kinds of children's literature

Even very young children enjoy poems. Nursery rhymes are short, simple poems. Some nursery rhymes are just for fun. Others teach the days of the week, the months of the year, the alphabet, and how to count.

People write other kinds of poems just for children. Many of these poems are funny or even silly. Some poems are about make-believe people and things, and some are about the real world. Some are about feelings.

People of all ages enjoy old stories, such as folk tales, fairy tales, and myths. Parents told these stories to their children long before they were written down. Later, their children passed them on to children of their own.

The stories are told very simply. They have action and colorful characters, and some of them are funny. Folk tales are stories about ordinary people. Fairy tales are about fairies, elves, and other make-believe people with special powers.

Folk tales and fairy tales come from many countries. One famous collection is *Grimm's Fairy Tales.* They are stories collected in Germany by

Mary, Mary, Quite Contrary is a nursery rhyme that children have enjoyed for many years.

Fairy tales are told and read to children in many different countries. *Lon Po Po* is a retelling of a Chinese fairy tale that is like "Little Red Riding Hood."

Jakob and Wilhelm Grimm. Another famous collection is the *Arabian Nights*. Hans Christian Andersen was a Danish author and storyteller. He wrote many delightful stories that are like folk tales.

Myths are ancient stories that try to explain why or how something happens, such as why the sun rises and sets. Myths also come from many lands.

Other old stories can be found in ballads and fables. Ballads are story-poems. They were often sung. Fables are short stories that teach a lesson about right and wrong. In many fables, the characters are animals that talk and think.

Fiction (*FIHK shuhn*) is one of the main kinds of writing for children. Fiction stories are not true. Writers make them up. Some of the stories are fantasies, or stories about things that could not really happen. Others are adventure stories and mystery stories. Some are about people in other countries and the way they live.

Historical fiction is about real times and events in history, but most of the characters are not real people. Science fiction is often about adventures that could take place in outer space, on other planets, or in the future.

Many stories are about people in everyday life. The stories show how people deal with their families and friends. The characters may have big problems, such as a death in the family.

Biographies (*by AHG ruh feez*) are another important kind of writing for children. Biographies are true stories about the lives of

Toad, a good-hearted but foolish animal, slowly learns the error of his ways in *The Wind in the Willows*. This classic children's book about the adventures of Toad, Rat, Mole, and other small animals dates back to 1908.

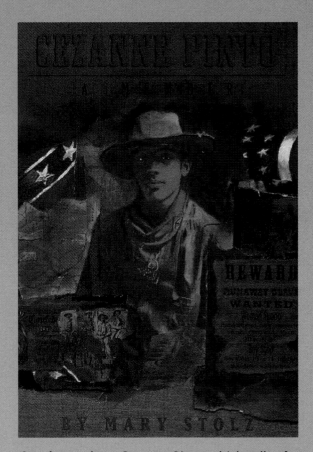

Stories such as *Cezanne Pinto*, which tells of a slave who escapes to Canada and becomes a cowboy, are historical fiction.

This nonfiction book uses detailed photographs to describe how dragonflies behave.

Pippi Longstocking is the story of a nine-year-old girl who has no parents but lives with her monkey, Mr. Nilsson, and her horse. Pippi is a strong, clever girl who has many adventures.

real people. The people may have made great discoveries, or been very brave, or created great art. Writers of biographies base their stories on facts.

Books of facts are called nonfiction (*nahn FIHK shuhn*). Nonfiction books may be about art, science, or history. Some books are about people in other cultures. Some are about problems, such as moving to a new neighborhood.

History of children's literature

People have told stories to children since ancient times. The first books written in English appeared about 1,400 years ago. They were written in verses and were meant to teach children. For almost 1,000 years, books for children were written that way.

In the 1600's, a teacher named Comenius made the first book with pictures for children. He thought books for children should entertain them as well as teach them.

From the 1500's to the 1800's, printers in England made books that cost very little. The books contained old tales and ballads. Grown-ups thought they were terrible, but children enjoyed them. In the late 1600's, the first book of Mother Goose verses was published in France.

During the 1700's, two books became favorites with both adults and children. One was *Gulliver's Travels* by Jonathan Swift. The other was *Robinson Crusoe* by Daniel Defoe. Then an English publisher named John Newbery published *A Little Pretty Pocket-Book*. It contained fables, games, rhymes, and songs especially for children.

In the 1800's, many people wrote books for children. Some are still favorites today. In England, Lewis Carroll wrote *Alice's Adventures in Wonderland* and *Through the Looking-Glass*. In the United States, Louisa May Alcott wrote *Little Women*, a story about an American family. Pictures began to be important.

More children's books were published in the 1900's than in all the hundreds of years before that. Picture books became favorites. *The Tale of Peter Rabbit*, by Beatrix Potter, was one of the first real picture books. The book first appeared with illustrations in 1902, and it is still a best-loved story. Magazines for children became popular, too.

Why Mosquitoes Buzz in People's Ears is an African folk tale. It explains a familiar happening in a fanciful way.

Some important awards, or prizes, are given for children's books. In the United States, the Caldecott Medal is given each year to an artist for the best picture book. The Newbery Award is given each year to a writer for the most outstanding book for children. In Canada, the best books in both English and French receive the Book of the Year for Children Award. Many groups and many countries now give prizes to people who write and illustrate books for children.

Other articles to read:

Aesop's Fables
Alcott, Louisa May
Arabian Nights
Arthur, King
Barrie, Sir James
Baum, L. Frank
Brooks, Gwendolyn
Bunyan, Paul
Carroll, Lewis
Cleary, Beverly
Dahl, Roald
Dickens, Charles
Fable
Fairy tale
Grimm brothers
Hamilton, Virginia
Hinton, S. E.
Konigsburg, Elaine
Lewis, C. S.
Longfellow, Henry Wadsworth

Milne, A. A.
Mother Goose
Mythology
Peter Pan
Pied Piper of Hamelin
Potter, Beatrix
Robin Hood
Robinson Crusoe
Sendak, Maurice
Seuss, Dr.
Stevenson, Robert Louis
Stine, R. L.
Swift, Jonathan
Twain, Mark
White, E. B.
Wilder, Laura Ingalls

Black Beauty tells the story of a horse that is hurt and treated unfairly by different owners, but finds happiness in the end. *Black Beauty* has been popular since it first appeared in 1877.

Lithuania

Lithuania (*lih thoo AY nee uh*) is a country in Europe. It lies on the shore of the Baltic Sea. It is bordered by Latvia, Belarus, Poland, and Russia. Vilnius is Lithuania's capital and largest city.

Much of Lithuania is made up of flat land. The country has about 3,000 small lakes and hundreds of rivers. Forests cover much of the land.

Most of the people of Lithuania come from Lithuanian families. They have their own way of life and their own language. Other groups in Lithuania include people from Russia, Poland, Belarus, and Ukraine. A small number of Jews also live in Lithuania.

More than half of Lithuania's workers have jobs in banks, schools, stores, and other places that provide services for people. Factories in Lithuania make prepared foods, appliances such as refrigerators, and other products. Many farmers raise beef and dairy cattle. The most important farm crops are barley and potatoes.

In the 1100's, Lithuanians joined into a single nation. In the 1300's, Lithuania and Poland were joined under the rule of one king. Russia took control of Lithuania in 1795. Lithuania was an independent country from 1918 to 1940. In 1940, the Soviet Union took control of Lithuania. When the Soviet Union broke up in 1991, Lithuania became an independent country again.

Facts About Lithuania

Capital: Vilnius.

Area: 25,174 sq. mi. (65,200 km²).

Population: Estimated 1998 population—3,696,000.

Official language: Lithuanian.

Climate: Cold winters and mild summers, with medium rainfall.

Chief products:

Agriculture: barley, beef cattle, chickens, dairy cattle, hogs, potatoes, sugar beets.

Manufacturing: appliances, chemicals, cloth, electrical equipment, food products, machinery, metal products, petroleum products, wood products.

Form of government: Republic.

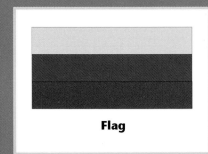

Flag

Lithuania and its neighbors

Little Dipper. See Big and Little Dippers.

Little League Baseball

Little League Baseball is an organization of baseball and softball programs for boys and girls. The boys and girls are from 5 to 18 years old. Both boys and girls may play in the baseball programs, but most of the players are boys. The softball programs are for girls only.

Each Little League team may have 12 to 15 players. Teams play at least 15 games each season to decide which is the best team. An all-star team, which includes the best players from each team, plays after the regular season.

The Little League program was developed by Carl Stotz and George and Bert Bebble in 1939.

Boys and girls between 5 and 18 years old play baseball on Little League teams.

Liver

The liver is the largest gland in the human body. A gland is an organ that produces chemicals. The liver is the body's main chemical factory. It also stores food.

The liver is reddish-brown. It is in the upper-right part of the abdomen (*AB duh muhn*), or belly, above the stomach and intestines. An adult's liver weighs about 3 pounds (1.4 kilograms).

The liver helps the body digest food. It makes bile, a liquid that helps break down fats. The liver also removes some digested food from the blood and stores it. Then, when the body needs the food, the liver puts it back into the blood. The liver also removes poisons and wastes from the blood and helps the body fight disease.

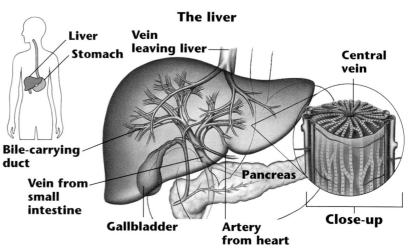

The liver

Liver
Stomach
Vein leaving liver
Central vein
Bile-carrying duct
Vein from small intestine
Pancreas
Gallbladder
Artery from heart
Close-up

Lizard

• •

Horned lizard

Beaded lizard

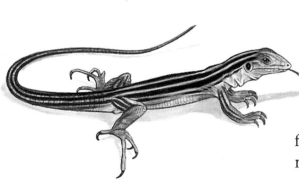

Six-lined race runner

Lizards are reptiles. They are closely related to snakes. The smallest lizards are only a few inches long. The largest lizards are the Komodo dragons of India. They grow up to 10 feet (3 meters) long.

Lizards are cold-blooded. The temperature of their bodies changes along with the temperature of their surroundings. So lizards are usually found in warm or hot places.

Most lizards live on the ground or in trees. Some climb trees with claws like a cat's. Some have toes like suction cups. These lizards can walk across ceilings and windows. Giant monitor lizards can swim. Flying dragons can spread out folds of skin and glide from tree to tree. However, they cannot really fly.

Some lizards escape from enemies by shedding their tails. The enemy gets the wiggling tail, while the lizard gets away. It simply grows a new tail. Other lizards hiss and lash their tails to scare off enemies. Some change color to blend with their surroundings and hide from their enemies. A few, such as monitor lizards, are fierce fighters.

Most lizards eat insects and small animals. But marine, or ocean, iguanas feed on small water plants called algae. Most lizards lay eggs, but a few kinds give birth to live young.

Human beings are a danger to some lizards. Some people hunt lizards, gather their eggs for food, and sell their skins for leather. Many countries now have laws against hunting lizards.

Other articles to read: **Chameleon; Flying dragon; Gila monster.**

Five-lined skink

Llama

Llamas (*LAH muhz*) are animals in the camel family. They and their relatives—alpacas, guanacos, and vicuñas—live in South America. Llamas look like small camels without humps. They are about 4 feet (1.2 meters) high at the shoulder. They have long, thick hair that may be tan, white, gray, or black. Llamas can carry heavy loads. They are good at walking on mountain trails. However, if a llama's pack is too heavy, or if the llama feels it has worked hard enough, it lies down and will not move.

American Indians use llamas to carry goods. They also get meat, wool, and leather from llamas. Some llamas are raised on farms in the United States and Canada.

Other articles to read: **Alpaca; Guanaco.**

Llamas

Lobster

Lobsters are animals that live on the ocean bottom. They are crustaceans (*kruhs TAY shuhnz*). Crustaceans have a hard shell, a body with sections, and jointed legs.

Lobsters' bodies have a head, a center section, and a tail. They also have five pairs of legs. American lobsters have heavy claws on the front pair of legs. They use these claws to kill other animals and tear their food apart. Lobsters eat clams, crabs, snails, small fish, and, sometimes, other lobsters.

The female lobster lays thousands of eggs at one time. They stick to her body until they hatch. As lobsters grow, they molt (*mohlt*), or shed their hard shell. They form a new, soft shell under the old one. Then they split the old shell and crawl out. They hide until the new shell hardens.

Many people think lobsters are delicious to eat. People catch them in the Atlantic and Pacific oceans.

Lobster

Loch Ness monster

The Loch Ness monster (*lahk NEHS MAHN stuhr*) is a large animal that some people believe lives in Loch Ness, a lake in northern Scotland. If there is such an animal, it prefers to stay away from people. However, hundreds of people claim to have seen the Loch Ness monster. The animal is said to have flippers, one or two humps, and a long, thin neck. Some people believe the animal may be related to a dinosaurlike reptile or to a modern sea animal.

The earliest known sighting of the Loch Ness monster dates back to the year 565. Since 1960, researchers have explored Loch Ness. So far, there is no proof that the Loch Ness monster is real.

The Loch Ness monster might look like this.

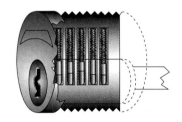

A pin-tumbler lock
in locked position

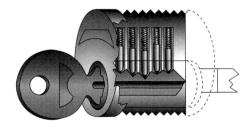

A key moves the tumblers to open the lock.

Lock

Locks are machines that prevent people from opening doors or other things. People use locks to protect themselves and the things they own.

Some kinds of locks are mechanical (*muh KAN uh kuhl*). That means they have moving parts that work without electricity.

Most mechanical locks have metal parts called tumblers. When the right key is put into the lock, it pushes the tumblers back. Then the key can turn part of the lock. As the part turns, it moves the bolt—the piece that keeps the lock shut. The bolt slides out of the way, and the lock opens.

Some kinds of locks are electric. One kind is opened with a special plastic card. The lock reads a code on the card. It sends the information to a computer. If the code on the card matches a code in the computer, the lock opens.

Another kind of electric lock opens with a combination of letters or numbers. People punch or dial the combination. If the combination matches one in a computer, the lock opens.

Some electric locks recognize people's fingerprints, eyes, voices, or other features. A scanner compares the feature, such as a fingerprint, with information in a computer. If they match, the lock opens.

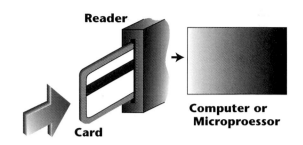

Reader

Card

Computer or Microproessor

Some locks open for the right code on a card.

Locomotive. See Railroad.

Locust

Locusts are a kind of grasshopper. They migrate, or move, from place to place. Locusts live on every continent except Antarctica.

Most locusts are about 2 inches (5 centimeters) long. They have a large head, large eyes, and short antennae, or feelers. Locusts have long hind legs and four wings. They can make a sound by rubbing their hind legs on their front wings.

Locusts migrate only after many females lay their eggs close together. When the young hatch, they stay together. They meet other groups of young locusts and form a swarm. Some swarms have millions of locusts. Wherever they land, they eat and destroy plants. A swarm can make as much noise as an airplane. It can be so thick that it shuts out the sunlight.

Locusts have been known since ancient times. One swarm in 1889 was believed to cover 2,000 square miles (5,200 square kilometers) by the Red Sea, which lies between southwestern Asia and northeastern Africa.

Some swarms have millions of locusts.

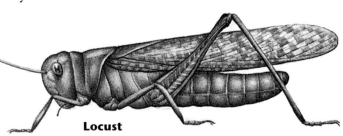

Locust

Log cabin

● ●

Log cabins were built by many early settlers in North America beginning in the 1600's. They could be built with very few tools.

The simplest cabins were made of round logs with curved notches, or cut-outs, near the ends. The first row of logs was laid on the ground. Then other rows were fitted on top of them. Each row of logs rested in the notches of the row underneath. The spaces between the logs were filled with stones or wood and sealed with mud.

People in Europe had built cabins for hundreds of years. Many different kinds of cabins were built in America. The settlers came from many different countries, and each group built cabins in its own

American settlers built log cabins.

style. Five American presidents—Andrew Jackson, James Polk, James Buchanan, Abraham Lincoln, and James Garfield—were born in log cabins.

Logging

Logging is the act of cutting down trees for lumber, or wood. Loggers are also called lumberjacks.

Before loggers go into the woods, a forester decides which trees they should cut. The forester is a scientist trained in taking care of forests. Foresters try to grow the kinds of trees that give the greatest amount of lumber.

Loggers called fallers cut down, or fell, the trees that the forester has marked for cutting. After a tree has been felled, workers called buckers cut up the tree trunks. This makes it easier to get the wood out of the forest.

Since the mid-1900's, large machines have done most of this work. For example, some machines can cut down a tree, remove its branches, cut it into logs, and gather the logs into bunches.

Taking the logs from the woods to the sawmill is the second step in logging. A sawmill is a place where logs are cut into lumber by machines. The loggers use tractors to skid, or drag, the logs to the landing—a central place in the woods. Then they use trucks to carry the logs from the landing to the sawmill.

At the sawmill, a moving chain carries the logs into the mill. In most mills, a log debarker removes the bark before the log reaches the first saw, called the headsaw. Large logs are moved onto a platform called a carriage, which carries them back and forth past the headsaw. Each time the carriage goes past the saw, the saw slices off a board. The boards are then trimmed and sorted by their quality, size, and kind of wood.

Tree trunks are cut in sections before leaving the forest.

Machines at a sawmill cut tree trunks into boards.

London

●●●●●●●●●●●●●●●●●●●●●●●●●●●●●●●●●●●

London is the capital of the United Kingdom of Great Britain and Northern Ireland. It is one of the world's oldest and largest cities. People have lived in London for about 2,000 years.

The River Thames (*tehmz*) flows east through the middle of London. Central London has three main sections. Two of the sections, the City and the West End, are on the north side of the river. The third section, the South Bank, is on the south side.

The City is the oldest part of London, but most of the old buildings were torn down to make room for modern offices and bank buildings. The West End is the center of Britain's government, and the towers of the Houses of Parliament are a familiar sight along the Thames. The West End is also famous for its many theaters and shopping districts, especially around Piccadilly Circus, where six busy streets come together. The South Bank has many office buildings and a large, modern cultural center.

Each year, millions of people visit London's many museums, parks, and well-known places such as Buckingham Palace and the Tower of London. Buckingham Palace is the London home of the British royal family. Long ago, the Tower of London was a prison, but now it holds the royal jewels. Soldiers in fancy red uniforms guard the palace and the tower.

Other articles to read: **Big Ben; Buckingham Palace; London Bridge; Tower of London.**

London and the Thames River

London Bridge

London Bridge is in London, England. It is one of London's 15 bridges across the River Thames (*tehmz*).

A new London Bridge was completed in 1973. It replaced the famous London Bridge that was built between 1823 and 1831. In 1967, workers took the old bridge apart. It was moved to Arizona and rebuilt in Lake Havasu City.

The first London Bridge was made of wood. It was built by the Romans and rebuilt several times. The first stone bridge was finished in 1209 and used until it was torn down in about 1832. It was the bridge in the nursery rhyme "London Bridge." The bridge had houses on both sides. Sometimes, when traitors were put to death, their heads were hung over the entrance.

Old London Bridge

Longfellow, Henry Wadsworth

Henry Wadsworth Longfellow

Henry Wadsworth Longfellow (1807-1882) was the most famous American poet of the 1800's. Many of his poems are among the most familiar in American literature. Longfellow's best-known longer works include *Evangeline* and *The Song of Hiawatha*. Among his popular shorter poems are "The Village Blacksmith," "The Children's Hour," and "Paul Revere's Ride."

Longfellow was born on February 27, 1807, in Portland, in what is now Maine. His first book of poems, *Voices of the Night,* appeared in 1839. *Evangeline: A Tale of Acadie* (1847) made Longfellow the most popular poet of his time.

Longfellow lived for many years in Craigie House in Cambridge, Massachusetts. Today, the house and grounds make up the Longfellow National Historic Site.

Longitude and latitude

Longitude and latitude are measurements used to locate any point on the earth. People who make maps use imaginary lines to divide the earth into sections. These lines are called meridians of longitude and parallels of latitude.

Meridians of longitude run north and south along the surface of the earth. Mapmakers think of the earth as a huge globe that is divided into 360 equal slices. Meridians of longitude divide the slices on the outside of the globe.

Parallels of latitude run east and west along the earth's surface. The equator is a parallel of latitude that circles the middle of the earth. The latitude of a point is measured by its distance from the equator.

Other articles to read: **Equator; Time.**

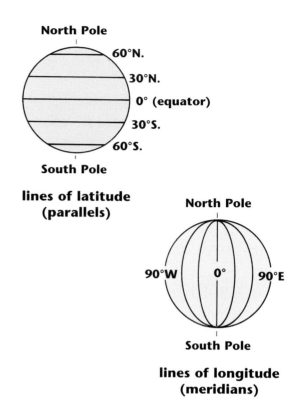

lines of latitude
(parallels)

lines of longitude
(meridians)

Nancy Lopez

Lopez, Nancy

Nancy Lopez (1957-   ) is one of the most popular players in the history of women's golf. She is the first person to win five tournaments in a row. She set the record in 1978.

Lopez was born in Torrance, California. When she was 12 years old, she won the New Mexico Women's Amateur title. After two years at Tulsa University in Tulsa, Oklahoma, she began playing professionally. In 1978, she won nine tournaments and was Rookie of the Year and Player of the Year. She has been one of the top 10 women golfers 13 times.

In 1987, Lopez became a member of the Ladies Professional Golf Association (LPGA) Hall of Fame.

Lorry. See Truck.

Los Angeles

● ●

Los Angeles is a huge city in southern California. It is on the Pacific Ocean. It is the second largest city in the United States, after New York.

Los Angeles is one of the fastest-growing cities in terms of people. It is also very large in land area. It has spread by taking in nearby cities and towns.

Los Angeles—especially the Hollywood district—is famous for making movies and television shows. Other industries in Los Angeles produce such products as airplanes, spacecraft, and computers. The city's people also work in banks, restaurants, hotels, and other businesses.

Los Angeles has many museums and theaters. It also has fine beaches and is close to mountain vacation spots.

Los Angeles has some big problems, too. For example, earthquakes there have caused a lot of damage. A shortage of open land and a serious problem with pollution are other concerns.

Los Angeles

Louisiana

● ●

Louisiana is one of the Southern States of the United States. It lies on the Gulf of Mexico between Mississippi and Texas. Arkansas lies to the north.

Louisiana is called the *Pelican State* for the brown pelicans that live along the coast. It is also known as the *Bayou State*. Bayous (*BY ooz*) are streams of slow-moving water.

Baton Rouge is the capital and second largest city of Louisiana. It lies close to where the Mississippi River empties into the Gulf of Mexico. It is a major U.S. port.

New Orleans, Louisiana's largest city, is one of the world's busiest seaports. It is famous for a celebration called Mardi Gras, held every year.

Land. Most of Louisiana is a low plain with rich, dark soil. The Mississippi Delta has the richest soil. It is the large area where the Mississippi River meets the Gulf of Mexico.

Sometimes the Mississippi and other rivers around the state overflow and cause flooding. The people of Louisiana have built special walls called *levees* to keep the water back.

Louisiana has many lakes, swamps, and marshes. Marshes are areas of land that are covered with water most of the time. Forests of cypress and oak trees are found in many parts of Louisiana.

Resources and products. Louisiana's rich soil is good for growing crops such as cotton, rice, sugar cane, soybeans, sweet potatoes, peaches, and strawberries. Chickens and beef and dairy cattle are also important in Louisiana.

Mining is a major industry in Louisiana. Oil and natural gas are the state's chief mineral products. Some of the gas comes from underwater fields in the Gulf of Mexico.

Trees in this bayou are covered with Spanish moss.

Baton Rouge

Louisiana (blue) ranks 31st in size among the states.

State flag

State seal

Factories make many products. Chemicals, such as medicine and fertilizer, are the chief products. Ships, trucks, and airplanes are also built in Louisiana.

France sold Louisiana to the United States in 1803 for about $15 million.

Important dates in Louisiana

Indian days	Indians lived in Louisiana long before the first Europeans arrived. They belonged to about 30 tribes, including the Atakapa, Caddo, Chitimacha, and Tunica.
1541	Hernando de Soto led a group of Spanish explorers into what is now Louisiana.
1682	French explorer Rene-Robert Cavelier, Sieur de la Salle, reached what is now Louisiana and claimed the area for France.
1699	The royal French colony of Louisiana was founded.
1718	The French governor of Louisiana, Jean Baptiste le Moyne, Sieur de Bienville, founded New Orleans.
1803	The U.S. purchased Louisiana from France.
1812	Louisiana became the 18th state on April 30.
1861	Louisiana left the United States and joined a group of Southern States called the Confederacy. The Confederacy lost to the United States in the Civil War (1861-1865).
1862	United States troops captured New Orleans.
1868	Louisiana became a U.S. state again. It adopted a new constitution that made slavery illegal and gave black people the right to vote.
Early 1900's	Jazz music probably began in New Orleans.
Early 1900's	People discovered deposits of oil and natural gas, two important sources of energy, in Louisiana.
1961	The Michoud Ordnance Plant (now Michoud Assembly Facility) in New Orleans started to produce Saturn rockets for space travel.
1975	A new state constitution went into effect.
1992	Hurricane Andrew struck Louisiana, killing 11 people and causing about $1 billion in damage.

Other articles to read: **Gulf of Mexico; Jazz; La Salle, Sieur de; Louisiana Purchase; Mississippi River; New Orleans.**

Facts About Louisiana

Capital: Baton Rouge

Area: 47,720 sq. mi. (123,593 km²).

Population: 4,238,216.

Year of statehood: 1812.

State abbreviations: La. (traditional), LA (postal).

State motto: *Union, Justice, and Confidence.*

State songs: "Give Me Louisiana" by Doralice Fontane. "You Are My Sunshine" by Jimmy H. Davis and Charles Mitchell.

Largest cities: New Orleans, Baton Rouge, Shreveport.

Government:
State government:
Governor: 4-year term.
State senators: 39; 4-year terms.
State representatives: 105; 4-year terms.
Parishes: 64.

Federal government:
U.S. senators: 2.
U.S. representatives: 7.
Electoral votes: 9.

State bird
Brown pelican

State flower
Magnolia

Louisiana Purchase

● ●

The Louisiana Purchase nearly doubled the size of the United States.

In the Louisiana Purchase, the United States bought a huge area of land from France in 1803 for about $15 million. This land, most of which was called the Louisiana Territory, extended from the Mississippi River to the Rocky Mountains. It nearly doubled the size of the United States.

For many years, Spain had owned the Louisiana Territory and the Floridas, which included Florida and land west to New Orleans. Americans stored many goods in New Orleans before they shipped them to other places to be sold. But beginning in 1798, Spain made it more difficult for Americans to store their goods. Then in 1800, France began to take control of the Floridas and the Louisiana Territory.

In 1803, U.S. President Thomas Jefferson sent messengers to France to try to buy the Floridas. The French offered to let the United States buy the Louisiana Territory and New Orleans. A treaty, or agreement, was signed in May 1803.

Louse

● ●

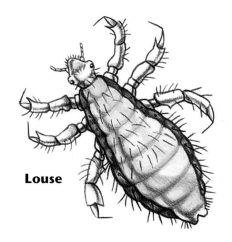

Louse

A louse is a small insect with no wings. Lice are parasites. They live and feed on birds and animals, including people. Lice cause itching, and they can spread disease.

There are two main kinds of lice. Chewing lice are often found on birds. They do not live on people.

Sucking lice live on an animal's skin. Several kinds live on people. Head lice pass from one person to another when people share combs or hats. Body lice lay eggs in clothing or bedding.

The best way to keep from getting lice is to keep your body clean and wear clean clothes. Drug stores sell special shampoos and lotions to kill lice.

Lucas, George

●●●●●●●●●●●●●●●●●●●●●●●●●●●●●●●

Geoorge Lucas (1944-   ) is an American motion-picture producer, director, and writer. He wrote and directed *Star Wars* (1977), a space-travel adventure and one of the most popular movies ever made. He also produced *Raiders of the Lost Ark* (1981), which featured an action-packed character called Indiana Jones.

Lucas was born in Modesto, California. He won a national student film contest in 1967. He was one of the authors and the director of *American Graffiti* (1973), a story about teen-agers.

Star Wars and two later films, *The Empire Strikes Back* (1980) and *Return of the Jedi* (1983), were successful in many countries. People liked the characters and enjoyed the special effects. Another film, *Star Wars Episode 1: The Phantom Menace* (1999) was about events that happened earlier than those in the first three films in the *Star Wars* series.

Lucas also produced two more movies about Indiana Jones (1984 and 1989), and *Willow* (1988).

George Lucas, *left,* with fellow director Steven Spielberg.

Lung

●●●●●●●●●●●●●●●●●●●●●●●●●●●●●●●

Lungs are important body parts, or organs. Lungs are the breathing organs of humans and other air-breathing animals. You have two lungs. They are inside your chest. When you breathe in and out, air goes in and out of your lungs. As blood flows through the lungs, it picks up oxygen from the air. The body needs oxygen to live. The blood also gets rid of a gas called carbon dioxide (*KAHR buhn dy AHK syd*) in the lungs. The body makes carbon dioxide as a waste material.

The lungs are like stretchy bags. They are filled with millions of tiny pockets of air called alveoli (*al VEE uh ly*).

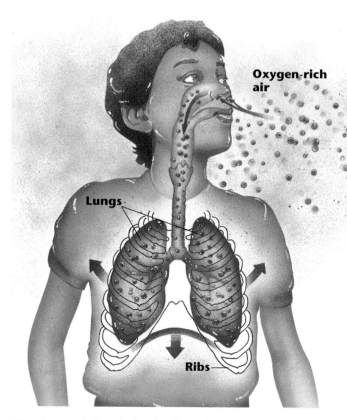

The lungs bring in fresh air and get rid of old air.

Air enters the body through the mouth and nose. It passes through the back of the nose and mouth and through the voice box. It then enters a system of tubes that leads to the alveoli in the lungs. These tubes are a lot like a tree, which divides into branches and twigs.

In order to give oxygen to the blood and remove carbon dioxide, the lungs must bring in fresh air and get rid of old air. Fresh air is brought in when the muscles in the chest wall cause the lungs to increase in size. When the muscles relax, the lungs become smaller again. Air flows out into the surrounding air.

Blood that has no oxygen in it is pumped by the heart into the walls of the alveoli. These walls are so thin that oxygen and carbon dioxide move through them easily. Oxygen passes from the alveoli to the blood. The blood travels back to the heart. The oxygen-filled blood is then pumped back to the different parts of the body.

The lungs do other things for the body as well. They protect the body from harmful "invaders," such as bacteria, viruses, and dust, that are mixed with the air. A sticky fluid called mucus lines the lungs and traps most of these things. Tiny, hairlike structures push the mucus upward into the throat. There, the mucus and any invaders are coughed up or swallowed. The lungs also help clean the blood. The air from the lungs helps us talk and make other sounds.

Other articles to read: **Asthma; Pneumonia; Respiration.**

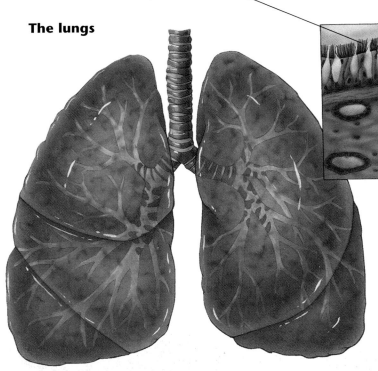

The lungs

Cilia sweep harmful particles out.

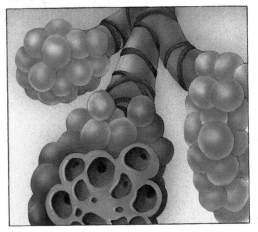

Old and fresh air change places in the alveoli.

Luther, Martin

● ●

Martin Luther (1483-1546) was a religious leader who brought about many changes in the Christian Church. Those changes were called the Reformation. The Reformation led to the beginning of Protestant churches.

Martin Luther was born on November 10, 1483, in the German town of Eisleben. He became a priest and a teacher in Wittenberg.

At the time, the Roman Catholic Church told people they could pay money to help make up for their sins, or mistakes. Luther believed that this church practice was wrong. He wrote a list of ninety-five reasons why he thought so and nailed them to a church door in Wittenberg.

Luther's list started a great argument in the church. Luther then questioned other things the church did. For example, he said that the pope and other church officials could make wrong judgments. He believed that God's teachings were in the Bible. These ideas were too different for the church to accept. In 1521, Luther was banned from the church, or kicked out.

Luther was asked to retract, or take back, his teachings, but he would not. That made him an outlaw. For a while, he was hidden by friends. Then he returned to Wittenberg. He wrote more papers explaining his beliefs. He also helped teach hundreds of pastors, or ministers, to bring his new ideas to the people.

By the time Luther died, a new church had formed. It was called the Lutheran Church. Luther was recognized as an important person for his powerful ideas about the Christian religion.

Martin Luther defending himself before Holy Roman Emperor Charles V in 1521.

Luxembourg

● ●

Luxembourg (*LUHK suhm BURG*) is one of Europe's oldest and smallest countries. It is bordered by Germany, France, and Belgium. The city of Luxembourg is the nation's capital and largest city.

The people of Luxembourg are like the people of Belgium, France, and Germany in some ways, but they value their own customs. They live better than many other Europeans. They use three languages: French, German, and Letzeburgesch. Letzeburgesch is a kind of German that many people use in everyday life.

Most of Luxembourg's people live in cities and towns. Most of the farms are in the southern part of the country. Farmers along the Moselle River grow grapes for wine.

Luxembourg is a leading maker of steel. The country once had many iron mines, but much less iron is mined today. The country now has factories for making computers. Companies also make products such as chemicals, plastics, and tires. Many people work in banking and in the businesses that help visitors to Luxembourg.

Luxembourg was an independent, or free, state more than 1,000 years ago. From the 1400's to the 1800's, it was ruled by several countries, including the Netherlands. Luxembourg became independent from the Netherlands in 1890. Germany controlled Luxembourg during part of World War I (1914-1918) and World War II (1939-1945). Today, Luxembourg is a member of the European Union (EU), a group that works to encourage cooperation among European nations. Many European countries are EU members, and some important EU offices are in Luxembourg.

Facts About Luxembourg

Capital: Luxembourg.

Area: 998 sq. mi. (2,586 km²).

Population: Estimated 1998 population—418,000.

Official languages: French, German, Letzeburgesch.

Climate: Mild and moist, with cold winters and cool summers.

Chief products:

Agriculture: barley, farm animals, grapes, oats, potatoes, wheat.

Mining: iron ore.

Manufacturing: chemicals, computers, plastics, steel, tires, wine.

Form of government: Constitutional monarchy. The country has an elected government and a grand duke or grand duchess as head of state.

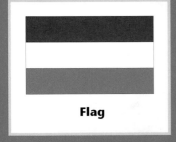

Flag

Luxembourg and its neighbors